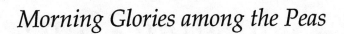

Morning Glories among the Peas

Morning Glories

among the Peas

A VIETNAM VETERAN'S STORY

BY

JAMES D. SEDDON

Iowa State University Press
AMES

© 1990 Iowa State University Press, Ames, Iowa 50010
All rights reserved

Manufactured in the United States of America
⊗ This book is printed on acid-free paper.

First edition, 1990

Library of Congress Cataloging-in-Publication Data

Seddon, James D.
    Morning glories among the peas : a Vietnam veteran's story / by James D. Seddon. — 1st ed.
        p.   cm.
    ISBN 0-8138-1398-0 (alk. paper). — ISBN 0-8138-1397-2 (pbk.)
        1. Vietnamese Conflict, 1961-1975—Personal narratives, American.
    2. Seddon, James D.   I. Title.
    DS559.5.S43   1990
    959.704'38—dc20   90-43477

This book is dedicated to my family: Patty, Shelley, and Heather.

It is also dedicated to Doc, Tom, and a young man I'll never know.

I love you all.

Where have you been, my son?
I've been to war, my father.
What did you learn, my son?
I learned to walk without my feet.
I learned to hear without my ears.
I learned to see without my eyes.
I learned to touch without my hands.
I learned to smell without my nose.
I learned to scream without my voice.
I learned to cry without my tears.
I learned to live without my soul.
That is what I learned, my father.
Welcome home, my son.

Preface

This book is not a historical account of the Vietnam War. It is not a record of battles won or lost, nor is it about economic or political ideals. I will leave that to the historians. *Morning Glories among the Peas* is a collection of emotions. It is about death and the fear of death. It is about life, prolonged pain, and lifelong scars. It is about failure and courage, strange love and strange hate. It is about smiles, tears, and memories. It is about the people of war, the mothers, fathers, grandparents, and children. It is about the lesser side of me, about the lesser side of all of us. Place these pages among the countless volumes of human history, and the next time someone speaks of war, remember them.

Acknowledgments

I owe a special thanks to Tim and Cathy Huisman, my brother-in-law and sister-in-law. I would also like to thank James P. Gannon and James S. Flansburg of the *Des Moines Sunday Register* and Bill Silag and Marilyn Keller of Iowa State University Press. With their help and encouragement, this book became a reality.

Where have you been, my son?

Fairfield, California—July 1968

One day before my twenty-second birthday, I stepped off an airplane at Travis Air Force Base, back into the world that raised me. I was home.

Everything was clean; everything was new; everything glittered and sparkled. There were so many bright colors that surely rainbows could no longer exist.

I walked from the plane to the terminal. At the door, a stern, gray-haired lady pointed toward the restroom and informed me that I must change my uniform. It was not authorized for wear in this country.

The restroom was very large and smelled of pine cleaner. The floor and walls were spotless, as was the row of mirrors along one wall. Down the center was a row of benches filled with GI's who had been given the same instructions.

I looked at myself in the mirror—bloodshot eyes, sunburned face, hair that no longer knew how to be combed. My jungle fatigues, wrinkled from three days' wear, were out of place in this neat, clean world.

I slowly unbuttoned my fatigue shirt, each stain and tattered edge reminding me of some no-name place I had been or of some horror I had seen. I removed the shirt, folded it neatly, and placed it on the bench.

I took from my suitcase a uniform that was acceptable by civilized standards. Before the mirror, a frog changed into a prince. When the transformation was complete, just as I started to pick up my fatigues, they were snatched from my hands by a man carrying a large trash bag. "You won't be needing this anymore, young man. You're back in the world."

With those words, he placed the fatigues—and a part of me—in the garbage. I didn't protest then, nor for eighteen more years.

The summers of my youth were spent with my brothers and sometimes a cousin or two. Like many Iowa boys, my days were filled with swimming in the pond and hoeing the garden, milking cows and eating corn on the cob. We built cabins and dug holes. At night, we slept under the big maple trees in the front yard. We played hide-and-seek and told ghost stories. If we were feeling especially brave, the graveyard down the road provided enough good healthy terror to keep us awake all night. My life was not only filled, it was fulfilling.

My father taught me the value and goodness of working with my hands. Together we built chicken houses and barns, added rooms to the house, and poured sidewalks. His stories and bits of wisdom accompanied our labors. They seemed unimportant then, but when added together have become a part of me.

My mother found security in fifty quarts of canned green beans. They meant something to eat on a cold winter day. A dozen freshly laid eggs or a bushel of new summer apples brought a smile to her face. She lived the Golden Rule and passed it on to her sons.

My parents never spoke of love. But, like morning glories among the peas, it was intertwined in all aspects of our lives. I was happy. I knew who I was. The glitter of the city was as foreign to me as the far-off war and the country that would redefine my life.

I've been to war, my father.

En route, Bangkok, Thailand, to Da Nang, Vietnam—
August 1967

My heart was keeping rhythm with the thump-thump of
the Jolly Green's main motor. As we broke through the clouds,
the air turned from cool to humid and hot. What had looked like
dark green carpet a few minutes before now revealed its true
form, a tangled jungle pocked with bomb craters.

Bill, the door gunner (I didn't know his last name), asked
me if I was scared. I told him I wasn't. But, in reality, I didn't *know*
how I felt. I know I had never felt like that before. It was nothing
like the nights in the graveyard when I was a kid.

The chopper shuddered and filled with smoke. I guessed
what had happened, but turned to Bill for confirmation. "We've
taken a few rounds, but don't worry," he said, with experience
in his voice. I grabbed Bill's arm as I reached for my flak jacket.
The chopper shuddered again, and I felt him pulling on me.
When I turned around, that arm was all that was left. In horror,
all I could think of was that I had to put it back—somehow, I had
to repair what had happened. "Before," things almost always
could be fixed.

I didn't know I was crying and yelling and shaking or that
I was still clutching that arm. From somewhere in the smoke,
someone pushed me into a seat along the side of the chopper,

grabbed the arm, and disappeared. I sat there with my hands growing stiff from dried blood.

> *Alfalfa, the smell of alfalfa and dust. My brothers and I were riding on the hay wagon taking bets on Buster Ewing's old Johnny-Popper. Could it make it up the next hill under the load of the baler and heavy hay wagons? We itched from the dirt that had stuck to our sweating bodies. Clouds were coming in fast from the southwest; another summer storm was brewing. We had to get the hay into the barn before it started raining.*

A raindrop ran from my forehead to the tip of my nose, tickling me awake, and reality returned. It had been two weeks since I had had any sleep. I walked, cried, and walked some more. I relived that day every day, trying to put in its proper place with the rest of my memories. There wasn't any niche where it fit.

Exhaustion is nature's way of saying "enough." Sleep has a way of redefining an emotional state. I finally fell asleep on a pile of sandbags at the far end of the flight line; a place that looked out on the part of the valley that Da Nang didn't inhabit. From a distance, the valley and surrounding mountains looked at peace with the world.

It was there that I started turning off the switches. The ones that make one care, hurt, love—until the only one left was marked "survive."

When my eyes turned from the green, lush valley to the barren tarmac of reality, I became a part of it, a part of the smells and the noise of mechanical madness, a part of despair.

> *The people of southern Iowa are cursed by an old-fashioned work ethic. Because of it they have been taken advantage of for the past hundred years. My great-great-grandfather, a blacklisted labor union organizer, had to leave England because he believed in a reasonable day's pay for an*

*honest day's work. He came to this country and found himself
in a hole, digging coal. When he died, he left a legacy of hard
work and a big hole in the ground, nothing more.*

*I grew up believing that hard work and honesty were the
most honored of all human virtues. I believed that if you
worked hard and were honest, you would be rewarded. I have
learned since then that I have control over the hard work, but
no control over the reward. Honesty works fine among people
who are honest, but it becomes synonymous with stupidity
when you are dealing with those who are not.*

I joined the Air Force with these Iowa values intact. Although I had basic philosophic differences with any organiza-
tion whose primary function was war, I was determined to do
the best job I could.

I became an aircraft mechanic, a good one. I followed
orders without question, which was a quality the military rewarded, and was assigned to a group of five young men who
dismantled crashed aircraft all over Southeast Asia—in the
middle of city streets, in jungle terrain where no man had ever
walked, we salvaged what we could and blew up what we
couldn't.

Sometimes we found ourselves in areas where our presence was contrary to U.S. foreign policy. We did a lot of work in
Cambodia and Laos, while the public was being told we weren't
there. We were a part of Uncle Sam's eyes and ears in that part
of the world.

After a time, our tiny band gained a small amount of
attention by those in high places. Uncle Sam has been accused of
a lot of things, but not taking advantage of a good thing isn't one
of them. For five months, we even traded our uniforms for
civilian clothes and gave up our military ID's for civilian ones.
We never stayed in one place long enough to arouse the curiosity
of those around us.

A part of, yet separate from, the rest of the armed forces, we
found ourselves out on a limb, in a tree that Uncle Sam claimed

not to own. We had become, in fact, a surveillance team as well as aircraft mechanics.

Cambodia-Vietnam border—September 1967

Steve looked at me and I looked back at him. An unspoken question passed between us, "What the hell are we doing here?" The sound of far-off thunder foretold some relief from the heat pressing down on us. Our feet were already wet, and it wouldn't be long before blisters would remind us to change our socks.

The world seemed extra quiet after the chopper left. Only the sound of birds settling in for a night's sleep broke the stillness. Our little band moved toward the tree line. Using only hand signals, we entered the dragon's den. The smell of decaying vegetation was stifling.

The jungle blocked what was left of the day's sunlight as we inched among the trees. Restless birds sounded our arrival. We stopped and had our last cigarette before a long night's crawl.

Mark, our lieutenant, motioned for Steve and me to take the point. Tom was behind us, and Doc was somewhere beyond that. Mark was in the rear, as far away from me as possible. A stickler for rules, he was pissed off at me because just before we left Da Nang I'd told a priest to get screwed. To me, military chaplains represented all the hypocrisy and pious simple-mindedness that had brought me to this place. At least I was honest with myself. I knew I had crossed the line that defined humanity, and I hated it. But *these* men tried to justify and sanctify what was taking place. God!

Somewhere to the west lay the Mekong River, about five kilometers. Then, another ten kilometers to the north was our goal, the city of Banam, Cambodia, on the east bank of the river. It sounded like a long crawl and a lot of work just to watch a bunch of boats go by.

The rain came, first in large drops popping on the leaves and then in pounding and deafening torrents, making the ground a murky cauldron. Steam rose. The moon surrendered what light it gave to flashes of lightning, and it was impossible to continue.

Steve had found a bush with large leaves that would shed some of the rain. I crawled in beside him. He asked, "Heard any good Polack jokes lately?"

"Not lately."

"Heard the one about the Polack soldier?"

"No."

"Well, don't laugh too hard, you're sitting beside one."

I laughed softly and patted his face, whispering, "You're all I've got." We sat back to back and spent the rest of the night talking about nothing and everything. Steve was my best friend. We shared ups and downs, dreams and fears. We had a language, and even an unspoken language, that only the two of us understood.

We talked of meeting after the war and doing something together. One day it was flying freight to South America, another it was farming in Iowa, and sometimes it was just watching the surf slap the rocks in northern California. But we both knew that it would never happen. When we were through there, we would go our separate ways.

Bird sounds filled the jungle, becoming louder and more intense as the sun turned the eastern sky from pale pink to brilliant red. All the insects in the world began their process of finding someone or something to pester. Slimy things started to creep, crawl, and slither over and around anything that inhabited their domain. As the sun warmed the ground, the smell of rotting vegetation insulted the nose of anyone not a part of this world.

Tom toppled our little poncho-covered pyramid, with a rough, "Get your asses up." He was a born soldier, if there is such a thing. He loved it; the muddier he got and the ranker he smelled, the better he liked it. Even when we weren't in the field, you could smell him coming around a corner. He wore his grungy uniform like a badge. No doubt about it, he longed to be a hero.

Mark appeared from behind a bush and advised us to eat something and be ready to move out in ten minutes. We had about six hours to reach the river on time. Six hours to cover twenty kilometers of sewer.

Steve and I once again had the privilege of pointing the way, the unknowing leading the unwilling. We were alert at the beginning of the day, but as time dragged on, everything became routine: look around and up and down, and keep walking. Nothing looked out of place. No sane person had ventured into this mess in a long time.

About noon, we stopped to suck down some water and eat something without taste or texture (the government called it meat). We checked our location with the map and noted our progress. We were about two kilometers behind schedule, time to quit screwing around and pick up the pace. I pulled off my boots, powdered my toes, changed my socks, and set off on another afternoon of adventure.

The map showed a small trail bordering the jungle at its termination to the east, then a band of rice fields before the jungle reappeared along the river. When we arrived at the jungle's edge, the trail looked like an interstate highway of mud. We faced a rice field that had not been planted in several years. Trees and weeds were reclaiming what had once been a fertile farm. Steve checked the map to see if we were in the right location and found that air recon had screwed up again. The map was at least two years old. A lot can change in two years, and there had been a lot of changes around there.

What now? Was the field mined? Was it booby-trapped? We didn't have a mine detector, and traps are hard to find. Mark, Tom, and Doc came up and a "what if" meeting was held. Since Mark had to make the final decision, he asked most of the questions. If we crossed the field, how many of us would be left at the other side? Should we try to learn what was going on there, or stick to our original mission? Would we have enough time to meet our ride out of the place if we ran into any trouble? Mark decided to risk it and check out the trail.

We marked our location on the map and started off. The jungle provided the protection we needed, so we walked along the tree line parallel with the trail. The farther we walked, the more apparent it became that we were in a serious situation. This was not a local byway. There were no cart tracks or buffalo prints. Instead, there were deep grooves made by heavily loaded trucks. And there had been a lot of them not too long ago.

The trail took a long, gradual turn to the left. As we slowly rounded the turn, the band of fields tapered off into jungle and the trail disappeared into the darkness under a canopy of trees. I stopped and waited for the rest to catch up.

"What's the matter?" Mark asked.

"I think we're getting in over our heads. This place looks too damn inviting for everyone but us. Someone is in there, and I don't think we want to know who it is."

I could tell that Mark was thinking the same thing. He was getting nervous, rubbing his hands together and tapping the ground with his foot.

"You're right, you're fuckin' right!" he agreed. "What do you think we ought to do?" His eyes looked down the trail, straining to see if the darkness would provide the answer. "Might as well go and see what's down there. It's better to know what we're up against. Doesn't mean we have to do anything about it." Everyone seemed to agree. Mark picked up his weapon. "Let's *do* it!"

Tom was running around goosing everyone while we were talking. When he heard the words, "Let's do it," he let out a war whoop. Everything was a game to him.

Mark grabbed him by the shirt sleeve and swung him around so he could look him in the face. "Look, you asshole, this is serious. I don't want to write a letter to your folks telling them how you got killed being a stupid jerk. You may want to be a hero, but the rest of us just want to get out of this place with our butts intact, so cut the crap."

I didn't pay much mind to what Tom did. It was just his way of relieving nervous energy. We all had a way of doing it. Steve played with his hat and smoked a lot. Doc tinkered with his weapon. I walked back and forth with my hands in my pockets, looking at the ground.

Tom took off and we each followed at ten-meter intervals. Our eyes studied every bush and intently examined the ground. Nothing was left to chance. Each step was made in slow motion, tenderly placing one foot softly in front of the other, making no sound. Carefully, ever so carefully, we moved. Time rushed by, but when we looked up to see how far we had come, the mouth of the jungle looked as far away as when we had started.

The sun had almost set when we reached the jungle entrance. Mark decided to send Tom and me ahead to recon the area, moving at a ninety-degree angle away from the trail for fifty meters, then fifty meters parallel with it, then coming back to where we started.

The trail had reached a large fan-shaped intersection with many smaller paths leading off in every direction. There didn't seem to be anyone around. Everything was quiet. Turning in circles and looking in every direction, Tom and I moved into the clearing. "Let's see what's down there," Tom said, pointing toward one of the paths.

Ten meters or so beyond us there was a clearing small enough not to interfere with the natural canopy the jungle provided. In the center was a ground-level log door about six feet square.

"This is a tunnel complex," I whispered to Tom. "Let's check it out."

"You first, I don't like dark holes."

"Chickenshit, give me a hand with this door," I growled. My eyes didn't adjust well to the darkness and it took a few seconds before a haphazard array of boxes and bags came into focus. I turned on a penlight and illuminated the tunnel with its contents barely enough to make out the items stored there. The printing on the boxes was Russian.

The construction of the boxes told me they contained some sort of ammunition. I pried the top corner loose from one of the larger crates stacked in the corner. Inside were rocket launchers. The bags contained rice and other types of dried food. All in all, there was enough stuff there for one hell of a party. It was time to get out of there.

When I was back on top, I told Tom what I had found. "Let's count the number of trails and take off," I said. We put the door back in place, covered our tracks, and hurried to report to Mark.

On the return walk sadness and melancholy began to temper and soften my fear. A new feeling emerged, a sense of loneliness, of desperation, of giving up. All the values, all the mind tools I had learned as a child, did not apply in this world. I wished that I could look in a mirror just to reassure myself that I was the same person.

Tears ran down my face, but I didn't know why. I was mad for feeling so helpless. There was no room for that kind of emotion in this place. It could get you killed. Yet I continued to struggle with a sense of who I was, not *what* I was. Separating the two was another war to fight. But I had to put the moment first, get through that day—survive.

When we arrived back, I sat down on a log and hung my head between my legs, exhausted. Steve put his hand on my shoulder to comfort me and asked, "What did you guys find up there?"

I began telling Mark what Tom and I had found. Tom filled in the parts I left out. When we were done, Mark's face showed anger and disbelief. He began rubbing his hands and walking in circles. "Screw it!" he snapped. "Let's just forget about this place. Mark it on the map, and make a note of it. Other than that, screw it. There isn't a goddamn thing we can do about what's there. Let's go to the river and watch the boats go by till our ride comes."

The walk to the river gave everyone a chance to unwind.

Steve walked beside me, not saying a word. Every once in a while, he would look at me out of the corner of his eye. After a long silence, he finally said, "If you want to talk, that's what these big ears are for. I'm not much older than you, but I've been around a lot. My mom says that I've been through more in my twenty-five years than most people. The one thing that I've learned is that there ain't nothing new. Things and people are always the same. We just ain't learned about them yet."

Steve was probably right. I had a lot of respect for his strengths and insight. If ever there was a man who should have had a lousy outlook on life, he was one. Born in a German concentration camp, he was hidden by his Polish father and Russian mother for six months, until the war was over, to keep the Germans from killing him. Then his father married his mother, and they moved to a relocation center in England. Although his father had been a college professor in Poland, he could find work only as a carpenter, while Steve's mother took in laundry.

In 1953, they emigrated to the United States and moved to New York. After many years of hard work, his father bought a seat on the New York Stock Exchange and became a wealthy man. But Steve still remembered the bad times. Nothing ever surprised him, especially when it came to human nature. He didn't expect too much.

The breeze was blowing down the river from the north, giving welcome relief from the heat. It didn't do that very often this time of year. The stars were shining in an ebony sky, and frogs were croaking along the river's edge. For a little while, it seemed to be a summer night in Iowa.

Dawn gave us our first good look at our home for the next three days. It could have been a park. A small knoll provided a clear view of the large bend in the river. We established a lookout and took turns watching the activities on the river.

There was a scattering of small fields along the river's edge, dark green from newly planted rice. When no river traffic was present, I watched the people work their tiny plots through my field glasses.

A farmer and his family appeared every morning at the same time, leading their water buffaloes with the smaller children riding on their backs in a small parade to the field. The family spent the day wading knee-deep in water, planting row after row of rice sprouts. My back hurt just watching them.

Unknown to Farmer Ho (my name for him, because he always carried a hoe), both he and I were kin of the land. Although he grew a different crop in a different world, I could relate to his problems and rewards. He brought a little bit of southern Iowa to this far-off, unfamiliar place.

The first day I watched the family at work, I noticed a four-wheel-drive truck drive by his field and slow as it passed the farmer and his wife. It then speeded up and drove off. When it was out of sight, Ho's wife ran to his side, and they began talking, with many hand gestures. I didn't pay much attention.

Shortly after noon on the second day, I relieved Steve and settled in to watch my little adopted family at work. The boat traffic was very slow. In fact, it seemed odd that it was so slack. I did notice a few small fishing boats that went from one bank to the other.

About two in the afternoon, the truck reappeared, moving more slowly than the day before. It stopped parallel with Ho and his wife. A man got out of the front seat and walked over to the farmer. I couldn't see what was taking place because the truck blocked my view. I did see the farmer's children start running toward their parents about the time two men in the back seat stood up.

What took place next will haunt me the rest of my life. There was a small puff of smoke and a distant sound of machine gun fire. A few seconds later, I could see my fears confirmed. They had shot the farmer and his wife!

The men in the jeep began to drive away. Farmer Ho lay face down in the mud. His wife was beside him on her back, rolling very slowly from side to side. About the time the children reached their parents, the jeep backed up. After another burst of gunfire, it sped away. Both parents lay dead, along with two of their children.

The three remaining children knelt beside their dead brother, sister, and parents. They pushed and pulled at their bodies, trying in vain to rouse them. It took a few moments before the reality of what had happened became clear to them. When it did, they put their arms around each other. They were so young, so innocent. What crisis in the adult world warranted such an atrocity?

I stood up ever so slowly, as though waiting for my mind to catch up with my body. The disbelief and terror were more than I could accept. It had to be some sort of silent movie, some horrible trick that would soon be over. I waited for the actors to get up and take a bow.

Instead, the three small children started walking slowly toward their home, turning around every so often to look back at the rest of their family. Finally they began running, perhaps thinking if they could not see it, the nightmare would go away. They disappeared into the grove of trees at the edge of the field.

Farmer Ho and his wife and children lay in the afternoon sun. I wanted to jump up and run to them, to call for help, but I couldn't. I wanted the world to see what had happened there, but no one cared. I sat in shock and looked at the bodies of "my" little family. As darkness came, I heard Tom coming to relieve me. I said, "I've got something to do," and ran down to the field.

I dragged Ho and his family from the mud and placed them in a row along the edge of their tiny plot. I wiped the mud from their moonlit faces and hair and closed their eyes. For the first time in my life, I prayed.

My God, the God that had always been in the back of my mind. I had never believed that praying was important. My God was not a Christian God. Good and evil, heaven and hell are created by man, not God. It is up to each individual to determine his or her own destiny. Organized religion had seemed to me to be little more than a social function, created to maintain order among the masses, with God only an excuse. I have found holiness among those of little religion,

*and righteous hypocrisy among those who profess to be
religious. But that night, I felt an overpowering need to call
out, to pray. Not for the Ho family, and not for myself, but for
God the creator. Men were killing each other all over the
world in his name.*

"Where the hell have you been? What have you been up
to?" Mark asked, mad as hell when I got back to the area. When
I explained what had happened, he eased up, yet he couldn't
possibly understand how I felt.

I poured a cup of coffee and settled back against a tree, then
closed my eyes and tried to black out the world. Mark came over,
kicked my foot, and asked, "Who were those guys down there
this afternoon? What were they dressed like?"

I opened my eyes. "I don't know. They were dressed like
anyone would dress around here."

"What kind of weapons did they have?"

"Automatic, that's all I know. Small caliber. Can I get some
sleep now?"

Mark took a deep breath. "You'd better. You've got Doc's
watch tonight. His leg is infected and he's running a fever."

"Where is he?" I asked, getting up.

Mark pointed toward a clump of bushes and said, "Over
there." Doc didn't look too good. He was pale and sweat beaded
his face. He had cut his leg falling on a sharp stick the day before.

"Don't feel too good, huh? How bad is it?" I rolled back his
pant leg, exposing the bandage that covered a leg twice normal
size.

"Looks pretty gross, doesn't it?" Doc asked.

"I'm no expert, but I'd keep a close eye on it. Don't worry,
we'll get you out of here. Just lay back and relax." I ruffled his
hair and went over to Mark. "This kind of changes things,
doesn't it? He's pretty messed up."

Mark was looking down at the ground. "The chopper is
coming tomorrow afternoon. We'll never make it in time carrying Doc, even if we left now. I want you and Steve to check out

the river in the morning. See if you can find a boat."

I took a map when I went to relieve Tom, and Steve tagged along. If we were going to do something, we knew we'd better start planning it then. We were fifty kilometers, as the crow flies, upriver from the Vietnam border and about twice that far if we followed the river. Unless we could find a boat with a motor, it would take a week to get out of there, and Doc couldn't wait that long.

Steve and I decided to start checking the river before sunrise. If we did find a boat, we wanted to take off before anyone was awake. I started back to tell Mark our plan, and was halfway down the trail when the distant rumble of large trucks caught my attention. "Fuck, just what we need!" I thought.

When I got back to the area, Mark was already aware of the trucks. "Let's go see what's going on," he said, motioning to Tom and me. "First go get Steve. Have him come and keep an eye on Doc." Tom went to retrieve Steve. Mark and I checked our weapons while we waited.

The trucks had moved close by but were running with no lights, so it was hard to tell exactly where they were. The moon was not cooperating, and it was beginning to cloud up. When the moon came from behind one of the clouds, the silhouettes of ten large trucks appeared, moving slowly up the trail. I nudged Mark and said, "It's about time for Steve and me to get out of here, isn't it?"

"Yeah, go ahead, but be careful. There's got to be a bunch of boats on the river tonight. Plus a lot of people'll be moving around. Someone had to unload all this stuff."

Steve was sitting beside Doc when I got back to the area. They were talking about water skiing. "Doc says he wants to ski down the river," Steve joked. "He says he's pretty good on one ski."

"Why not? Sounds like a good cover. Maybe everyone will think we're a bunch of dumb 'round eyes' just out having a good time."

We left Doc and headed to the river. Neither Steve nor I had any idea where we might find a boat. All we knew was that most rivers had boats.

"Let's check this way," Steve said, motioning to his left. "I feel lucky."

"Sounds good to me."

We walked along the riverbank in the darkness. It smelled like any river, anywhere in the world, and it made the same swooshing sound as the water washed against the bank and the moonlight caught the waves.

"What kind of fish do you think we'd catch if we had the time?"

"Slick, smelly ones that flop around a lot when you take them out of the water. At least that's the only kind I ever caught," Steve said.

We hadn't walked too far when our ears caught the dull sound of wood bumping against wood, the sound a boat makes when it bounces against a dock. Straining our eyes in the darkness, we saw the outline of a boat. It was about twenty feet long, with a canopy in the middle. If it had a motor and a trailer and plenty of gas, we would be in business.

"Let's have a look," Steve said, as he moved toward the boat.

I grabbed hold of him. "Let's be careful. Sometimes they live aboard these things." As we got closer to the boat, the smell of dead fish filled the air.

"If anyone lives on this damn thing, their noses don't work. The smell is bad enough to make a fish want to take a bath." Steve never could stand bad smells.

"Let's go out and sit on the dock for a little while and see if we can hear anything. People usually make some kind of noise even when they're asleep. I've spent enough time with you guys to know that. Then if we don't hear anything, we'll take a look inside." Steve agreed, so we moved slowly to the end of the dock, next to the boat. Every sound intensifies when you are listening hard. It's as though the volume on the whole world is turned up, and even background noises that are usually ignored begin to play on the mind.

Steve stood up and announced, "Well, I've waited long enough. Let's have a look. You go to the other end and shine your flashlight in, and I'll look in from this end."

"Okay," I said reluctantly.

I saw the boat tip as Steve climbed aboard. A moment later, I bent around and directed my light under the canopy. There was nothing but a pile of fishing nets.

Steve said, "I bet the smell would go away if we threw these nets overboard."

"Yeah, but let's wait until we get downriver a little way," I said with relief.

Mark and Tom were ready to move when we got back. They had made a stretcher out of a couple of coats and two poles. Doc was lying on it ready to go.

"We've found a boat. About twenty minutes from here, about forty packing Doc. We checked it out, and it's got a motor and plenty of gas," Steve reported to Mark.

"Well, then let's get the hell out of here. You and Tom take Doc," Mark said, motioning to me.

The hike back to the river was welcome after wandering around that godforsaken place for five days. It was the first thing that made any sense. Maybe on the way downriver, I thought, we could figure out what we were doing there. And, when we got back, headquarters might be able to fill in the blanks.

Mark had another decision to make on our way to the boat: Should we try to sneak out of there and hide if we encountered another boat, or just blast down the river like we owned it, hoping to get across the border before anyone knew what we'd been up to? He decided to take a chance and go for it. We'd act like we owned the river.

We loaded Doc on board, threw our gear on, and shoved off. It was decided to let the current carry us for a distance before we started the engine. When we reached midstream, Steve cranked the engine to life and we were off. The old tub wouldn't set any speed records and the accommodations were pretty rough, but it was the sweetest trip we had taken in a long time. As the sun rose on the new day, the boat and its tattered crew had both settled into the rhythm of the river. At sunrise, everything always seems peaceful and fresh. Doc was getting worse, though. He drifted in and out of consciousness and was burning with fever. His leg was varying shades of purple and dark red. The tourniquet had not helped keep the poison from spreading to the rest of his body. Nobody talked about it, but everyone knew he was running a race with time.

The sun's reflections sparkled in the water and a cool breeze ruffled the boat's canopy. With the morning half gone, it had been uneventful. Each time we encountered another boat, we went to the other side of the river, as far away as we could get. Hidden under the canopy, we hoped no one would notice who we were. We knew in three more hours, we'd be home free.

What a wretched band we were—no one talking, looking off in different directions, everyone caught up in his own world, escaping reality, dreaming of where he would like to be.

Steve sat cradling Doc's head in his lap, every so often wiping his face with a wet T-shirt. Once in a while, he bent over and said something to Doc, or Doc whispered to him.

Doc always had a half smile on his face, like he knew something the rest of the world didn't. He was older than the rest of us, a sort of father figure and the calming element among us. We called him Doc not because he was a medic but because he had a Ph.D. He said he knew all the worthless information in the world—if you wanted to know anything worthless, just ask him, he was a philosopher. When we asked him why he took such a lowly job in the military when he could have had a commission, he said he wanted to be with real people. I didn't know what he meant by that when I first met him. But, the longer I was around him, the more I understood. There have always been a few men who looked at the mysteries of humankind and asked the question, Why? They come up with reasons and answers, but humanity doesn't listen, continuing to make the same mistakes over and over. Doc had burned out and given up on humanity. To him life was an ironic comedy.

Finally, in the distance, we heard the growling sound of a high-powered motor followed by the familiar outline of a U.S. Navy river patrol boat. We waved them alongside, told them who we were, and they threw us a line. We were home.

They put Doc in a pickup to drive him to the hospital.

Da Nang, Vietnam—late September 1967

The rest of us caught a Huey and headed back to Da Nang. "You guys unload the gear while I check in," Mark said as he headed for the ops building. "I'll find out where they took Doc." We had all the gear stacked on the flight line, leaning back against it trying to catch a few winks when Mark got back.

"Ready for a beer, boss?" Steve said.

Mark looked at us and said, "Doc's dead. He had a blood clot in his leg. When we moved him, it came loose and lodged in his brain. He died before they got him to the hospital."

Not saying anything, we all just wandered away. Mark was left standing beside the pile of gear. Then I turned around and said, "I'll get everybody together. See you in the morning."

I walked to the end of the flight line and looked at the mountains. I had to put Doc's death out of my mind somehow. The events of the past two days had brought me to a breaking point. I couldn't handle any more. One of the little switches had to be turned off, or they would be sending me home in a funny-looking jacket with extra-long sleeves that tie behind your back. So Jack Daniels and I spent the night together.

Doc had always said that death was the big payoff. Either he would have all the answers or it wouldn't matter. He said that in his line of work, death was the ultimate enigma. I hoped he had found all the answers, because he had left me with the gift of thinking and questioning. It is the only true freedom.

I found Steve sitting in the cafeteria. He and Tom were fiddling with cups of coffee, neither one of them aware of the rest of the world. They blankly stared at their cups. I sat down between them and looked at them without saying a word. I knew pretty much what was going through their minds and joined them in their blank world.

Tom broke the silence and asked, "What happened? What kind of place is this? I don't belong here. I don't have what it takes to live this way."

I looked at Tom. "This isn't living. It's just getting by. When someone starts thinking this is life, it's time to ship them to someplace where they can't harm themselves or other people. Tom, as long as you feel the way you do, you're normal."

Doc and I had talked for long hours about "the rules,"
as he used to call all the bullshit thrown at us from the day we
are born until the day we die. He found humor in most of it.
He said that if people wouldn't worry so much about follow-
ing the rules, they would have more time to be human. I tried
to understand what he meant.

In the fall of my fourteenth year, I did what most young
men in southern Iowa do. I went hunting. With a pocketful of
shells and my old twenty-two, I set off to stalk the wild beasts
of Valentine's woods. A small creek meandered through the
greenery and several meadows lined the creek's banks.

The woods and meadows were alive with squirrels and
rabbits. The creek's deeper holes were home for hundreds of
minnows. Birds of every color flew from oak to maple to ash in
their hurry to raise a family before the frost. During the
course of my childhood, I had come to know every inch of these
woods. I felt a part of them.

After looking for animal dens along the creek bank for a
while, I sat down on a limestone outcrop and turned my
attention to other game. As I sat there, a red-headed

*woodpecker flew into the woods with a loud squawk,
interrupting my tranquil world. Although he was at least a
hundred yards away, I drew a bead on him. I fired, and to my
surprise, the bird fell from the tree. I ran and picked him up—
shot right through the eye. The woods were at last quiet, but I
had never felt so out of place and I never again tried to prove
myself at the expense of another creature.*

    *Thinking on my own was a good feeling. I didn't have to
earn acceptance by conforming to the rest of the world. I had
been raised to follow the rules, to be a good citizen, and obey
the laws of my government and follow the morals of society. I
had always thought that laws and morals applied to everyone
in the same way and were for the good of everyone, that they
were the way people aspired to the loftier ideals of mankind,
with the hope of improving the lives of all. I have found since
that societies can be evil. They can go against all that is good.
They seem to be self-serving and selfish, ruled in one form or
another by self-serving, selfish people. People like myself
become unwilling tools of the society. Loving and caring for
some reason cannot be universally applied by the human
mind. Rules get in the way.*

Mark came walking into the cafeteria and informed us that
our presence was required at operations for a debriefing. We
entered Colonel Blane's office, a ragtag bunch of unmilitary
renegades. The colonel looked over his half-glasses and motioned to the conference room with his eyes. I could tell by his
expression that he wasn't happy. I really didn't care. We each
took a seat around the long conference table in the wood-
paneled room. Pictures of aircraft, tanks, and other armored
equipment lined the walls. The table had shiny glass ashtrays
and yellow notepads with freshly sharpened pencils lying neatly
on top.

    We were all slouched in our chairs when the colonel
walked into the room. Military protocol says we must come to
attention when an officer enters the room. But we didn't feel like

it, and he was even more pissed. He went to the head of the table, laid down his papers and glasses, and said, "I understand we ran into a little trouble out there. Captain, you want to fill me in?"

There was a long silence. Mark looked at each of us, gathering his thoughts, and answered, "Doc's dead, and there's a whole bunch of shit buried in the ground over there. Enough to blow the southern half of this fucking country into the South China Sea, and it's coming downriver. It's all in this report." He threw it across the table to the colonel. "If there're any questions about it, you know where to find me." He got up and walked out of the room. The colonel was saying something about his not being relieved as the door slammed.

"'Doc'—was that Thomas Allen Ryan?" the colonel asked, looking at Steve. Steve nodded yes.

"We'll see about getting a replacement."

I got out of my chair, turned around and looked at a picture of an F-4 hanging on the wall. "You can't replace Doc," I said. "He's only a blank to fill on your organizational chart, but to us he was somebody, a friend. So don't say you can replace him." Then I turned around, looked the colonel in the eyes, and said, "Do you UNDERSTAND?"

The colonel's face turned red, and he glared across the table at me and shouted, "Look, you wiseass, I was chasing Germans around Europe before you were *born*. I know what it's like to lose a buddy. I lost a lot of them. But I never forgot what my job was, and it was more important than anyone's life."

I glared back at him. "You're fucked, Colonel. If you understand, then, what the hell are you doing here? I'll tell you why. You feed your goddamn ego off this crap. So don't tell me your war stories. You *love* this stuff." I turned and walked out the door, while Tom and Steve traded glances.

Mark was standing in front of operations with his foot propped up on a large planter. His eyes were on the traffic in front of the building, but his mind was somewhere else. I fell in beside him.

"Fuck this place!" I said.

"Yeah," Mark responded in a low tone.

Tom and Steve came out the door a few minutes later. "That is one pissed-off colonel," Steve said as they settled in beside Mark and me.

"He'll get over it," Mark said. "If he doesn't, we'll get over it." We all walked away from the building toward the flight line. It was time to get the hell out of there for a while.

Bangkok, Thailand—October 1967

Mark had to stick around Da Nang for a few days and tie up loose ends. The rest of us caught the next flight to Bangkok. All we had on our minds was a beer, a bath, and a soft bed. Steve had married a Thai, a nice lady. He had called ahead for Kay and her little girl to meet us there. She would have our rooms ready. Kay's daughter, Bong, reveled in three daddies as long as we were around. It was as close to home as we could get.

The first night back, we each ate a big steak and drank most of the beer in Bangkok. When we left the restaurant, there was still a steak for Doc on the table, untouched. He would have gotten a kick out of it. Tom and I talked about taking the bikes up into the teak country the next day. He was from northern California, and the big trees reminded him of home. I was fascinated by the elephants that moved the large teak logs around. Such slow-moving grace and intelligence seemed out of place in an animal so large.

When we woke up the next day, we found out that it was already afternoon, and the beer from the night before had done something to the sun. It was so bright that it hurt my eyes, and I could tell it had the same effect on Tom. He hadn't come out from underneath the blankets, and from what he was saying, I didn't expect him to appear anytime soon. I went into the bathroom darkness and fumbled for the shower faucet, hoping the cold water would bring some relief, putting my eyeballs back in their sockets and shrinking my head to its original size. The rest of my body appeared to be intact, if not functional.

Since the sun was having a bad day, Tom and I decided to postpone our trip until the following morning. Instead, we tagged along with Steve and Kay while they did family things. We shopped for new clothes and daydreamed in front of store windows. The temptation of an ice cream parlor was more than we could stand. We stole Bong from her parents, adopted another half dozen street kids, and ate the place empty.

The next morning the sound of tires on wet pavement informed us that it was not likely to be the best day for a bike ride. But when the sun finally decided to cooperate, Tom and I loaded the bikes with the necessities (beer) and took off for the teak forests.

The highway was crowded with buses and brightly painted trucks. Taxis zipped in and out and around everything on the road. As we left the city, the traffic thinned and the road became a pleasure to drive. The flat rice fields around Bangkok slowly gave way to mountain forests. The highway wandered along rivers and valleys as it snaked its way north.

A motorcycle becomes an extension of its rider's personality. It sways and leans with the rider's moods. Tom and I were cruising, leaning with the curves, lying back with the wind in our faces, the smells and colors soothing our senses. We played with the road, speeding up and slowing down as the whim struck us. We stopped at waterfalls and fields of flowers, savoring the beauty, clearing human ways from our mind.

High in the mountains, a mist dripped from each leaf and twig, invaded every valley and crevice, created wispy planes from mountaintop to mountaintop. Cradled in the heart of the valley, a monastery's muffled, mournful gong summoned orange-robed monks from their velvet fields. In the mist, in the side of the mountain, a huge golden Buddha sat in a gazebo temple, smiling down on his flock. Time had stopped here, or perhaps, time had never existed here.

It was the kind of place that pulled you into the heart of its being. Our tension was replaced with a feeling of peace. It was the most natural urge in the world to follow the red path to the monastery and never return. But the world hardened its grip, and I turned to Tom and said, "Let's go."

By midmorning, the coolness of the teak forests brought relief from the heat. The huge trees towered above the forest floor. Vines connected the treetops into a tangled network that blocked the sun. Ferns and mosses of many colors and sizes made it impossible to venture very far from established paths. Tom and I rode slowly, absorbing the wonder and tranquility.

At a clearing along the side of the road, we pulled the bikes into the shade and settled down to enjoy it.

"It's funny how one forest can be so different from another. This place is not that far away from where we were the other day, but it's entirely different. I think it has more to do with the creatures that live here, if you get what I mean," I said.

"You know," Tom said, "I did a lot of thinking on our way up here this morning. I'm awful tired of fucking things up. I want to be like those monks down the mountain. I'm going to shave my head, find a cave on a mountaintop, and try to figure out what this life is all about. If anyone comes around and wants to know what I've learned, I'll tell them to get the hell off my mountain."

"It'll probably be some asshole trying to make a buck or subdivide the place," I laughed.

I asked Tom, "Do you ever get the feeling that you may be screwed up for life? That when you get home, the world will all be different, or that you'll be so changed you won't fit in anymore. I think about home, and it seems like a dream. I look at myself and wonder, who the hell are you? Two years ago, I had the world by the tail and was ready to show everyone that I had all the answers. But, now it seems like all I have is questions."

Tom looked at me for a while and said, "Don't think so much. Let's hit the road."

The rest of the day, we explored side trails and drank beer with the Thai loggers. We rode back to Bangkok in the coolness of the evening, stopping at the monastery to see if it had changed after sundown. It hadn't.

Steve came to our room the next morning and informed us that plans had been changed. Mark wanted us in Saigon the day after next. We were to meet him at the American embassy. We had never been so honored. Shit!

I remembered that I had some shirts to pick up at one of the tailor shops, so I decided to spend the day seeing some of the sights. I was feeling sorry for myself because it had been a long time since the last payday and the trip to the teak forests had just about tapped me dry. But Bangkok is a beautiful city and a lot can be enjoyed with very little money.

As I walked along the floating markets, a lady carrying a small child touched me on the shoulder. When I turned around, she asked if I could give her any money. People in Thailand were always begging money from Americans, so without thinking, I said I didn't have any to spare. She hung her head and began to walk away. As she was leaving, I noticed that she had a limp and a closer look revealed that her left foot was nothing but one big open sore. I caught up with her and gave her all the money I had in my pocket. I haven't ever spent money so wisely. My two shirts are probably still in that tailor shop in Bangkok.

Saigon, Vietnam—mid-October 1967

In Saigon, a different kind of war was being waged. There was very little fighting, but you could tell from the activity on the streets that someone was mad. The military was all over the place. Convoys of trucks and armored equipment held up traffic on just about any major street. Soldiers were everywhere, guarding everything. It was a tidy war. All the soldiers and equipment were crisp and clean. They were putting on a good show for the big shots who were all over the place.

The American embassy was a large white building. The trees that surrounded it hid how large it was. Steve, Tom, and I, like three farm boys visiting the city for the first time, stared at everything in awe and seemed to be in everyone's way as they hurried to get whatever they were doing done.

"We don't belong here," I said to them. "I wonder what Mark wants us here for?"

The guards at the embassy gate checked our security badges and let us in the compound. Finding Mark didn't prove to be much of a problem. He was waiting for us in the main lobby.

"We've got another job as soon as I get this Cambodia thing out of my hair. I'll know more after this meeting—some State Department guys want to know what's going on. I guess they can't read reports, want it from the horse's mouth. You guys just hang around until the meeting's over."

We all went down to the cafeteria. "Does anyone wear anything but white shirts and shiny black shoes?" Steve laughed, as he looked around the room. For some reason, all those people running around looking important was funny to us. Perhaps they *were* important, and it was the irony that we saw in all of it— this was where the serious shit came from, and no one *ever* got dirty.

Mark wandered into the cafeteria, looking around to see if his misfit crew had left the place intact. There was a relief on his face when he spotted us in a far corner being good boys. "How about you guys buy the boss a beer and I'll tell you something that'll curl your hair. But let's get the hell out of this place," he said as he pulled the chair out from under me.

We found a quiet bar along the street, sat down, and waited for Mark to finish his beer.

"Well, are you going to tell us what's going on, or do we have to sit here all day?" asked Steve. He got nervous when he had to wait too long.

Mark slid back away from the table a little and, with a half-laugh, started in: "You know, those people live in a different world. The report that I filed was just a little piece of the great big picture that those people don't want to look at. They don't want to believe that a bunch of guys up north can fight a war, let alone whip our asses. They're afraid of what the people back home are going to say. They keep thinking that we'll be out of here next week, or next month, because that's what they keep telling the politicians back home. Just send us a few more bucks and we'll have this mess cleared up in no time. But they know it really ain't going to happen. I sat in that room and had all these questions shot at me, and when they heard something they didn't like, all hell would break loose. They're playing a game with time up there, and time's running out. I've got a real cold feeling the government doesn't know what to do.

"Anyway, the long and the short of it is that we've got to go back to Da Nang and meet with this recon outfit made up of army and marine forces, get what info they have, come back down here, and meet with this bunch again. Then we're going back to Cambodia, is what it all boils down to. Laos and Cambodia are about to come apart, and the government wants as much information as possible on what's going on over there."

"What the hell do they expect from us?" I asked. "I don't know about you guys, but I didn't sign any papers saying that I'd take part in anything like this. I don't have the training or the know-how to do what they want. This whole mess is getting out of hand. I joined the air force to get *out* of this kind of shit. The idea of crawling around in a jungle looking for someone to shoot me doesn't make sense. But, here I am, listening to you say that's what I'm going to be doing for the foreseeable future. No way! Those guys upstairs have no idea what they're doing and until they can come up with a better reason than the one they've got, count me out. Hell, I'm liable to have my ass shot off before they decide that the whole thing isn't worth it! My ass is worth more than that. They can't say a damn thing if we tell them to shove it—we're not supposed to be there anyway. If those fuckers think it's so goddamn important, let's go get a couple of *them* and let them tag along. They can get the information they want firsthand."

Mark laughed. "Cool it, don't go off half-cocked. They don't want us to go traipsing around the country. We'd stick out like a sore thumb. They want us to work the edges, take the pulse of the people without them knowing it. Then we feed the info back to this place. We're not going to be there the rest of our lives, maybe six weeks, just long enough to get some kind of idea of what's going on so the big boys upstairs won't be surprised if the whole place blows."

I was still upset, "I don't trust the fuckers. Until they can give us the whole story of why we're going back to Cambodia, I don't want any part of it. You know as well as I that they always fill in the blanks after the fact. Hell, we don't know why we were there the last time. This time, I'm going to know what's going on up front. I'll just go back to Thailand and turn wrenches and Uncle Sam can't say a damn thing and he knows it. Hell, for the record, I'm AWOL right now."

"That's right," Mark said, "and don't think Uncle Sam doesn't know that, too. When you signed on the dotted line, you're his for four years. He can make you a hero or put you behind bars, all with the stroke of the old ballpoint, so don't zig too much when he zags, if you get what I mean. We'll get ours; paybacks are hell. As for the last time we were there, I finally got the full story on what was going through their stale minds. I guess there's been a lot of activity down in the Delta. Charley has been getting brave, making a lot of raids, and sticking around a lot longer than he used to. The few that *have* been caught are a different breed. They aren't local, come from up north. The government thinks that the Viet Cong have made a deal with somebody in the Cambodian government; Phnom Penh isn't too stable. When we get done in Da Nang, we'll have a better idea of what the whole picture is."

I was finding out firsthand that there are few rules in war, and they are subject to change at any moment. Rules are

*a desperate attempt to maintain some kind of order in a
situation that defies order. As long as there are rules, we can
still call ourselves civilized even though we are killing each
other.*
    *But the United States was breaking the rules. The
government was telling the public one thing and doing
another. It gave the impression that we were fighting this war
with honor and dignity, like all the other wars. The other guy
does all the nasty stuff. I can't say for certain what this
country did in other wars, but I doubt that things were much
different. I did know how they were fighting this war, and I
felt betrayed. If what I was doing had honor and was right,
then why didn't the people who had sent me here acknowledge
what was going on?*
    *I had a real fear of returning to Da Nang, but I didn't
know why. I had been there so many times in the past months
that it seemed as close to home as one could expect in that
situation. I believe it must have been a fear of what was going
to take place there. I was afraid I was going to take more
lessons in how not to be me. In the past few months, I had
begun to feel that an invisible ax had split me down the
middle. I was becoming two different people, and a person I
didn't like was winning, while the person I wanted to be just
stood by and watched helplessly. I was scared, scared of me.
The world was becoming a different place, and I was becoming
a part of it. The changes were subtle and sneaky, they crept in
and around, taking hold in whispers.*
    *I had to have control of every situation. Nothing could
be left to chance; everything and everyone was suspect. I
trusted only Mark, Tom, and Steve, and I trusted them with
my life. There was no rest, only fitful sleep where the pains of
the past were relived time after time. Time was always the
enemy; short periods dragged on forever, and days sometimes
flashed by and ran together in one blurry event. I had gaps in
my thinking, and my memory, gaps in time and sequence. The
job of staying alive became an obsession. Every nerve ending*

became raw from the intensity of the task. Slowly, reluctantly, grudgingly, I became a cog in the machine of war—a divided man, as divided as the country I was in.

There is something about fear that scars deeply. These scars bypass logic; they're unexplainable and personal. No two people are scarred in the same way. But everyone who lives through such insanity has them; it's just a matter of time before the fears grab hold and play hell with the mind. I've seen it in the faces of those just returned from the field, with their slow robot bodies moving from reflex not reason. Fear imbeds itself in the mind more firmly the more it is experienced. I feared fear.

What did you learn, my son?

Da Nang, Vietnam—October 1967

It was raining the day we returned to Da Nang, a slow gentle rain, the kind that can last for days. It was a rain that gets right down to business and cleans every cranny that previous rains forgot. It refreshes and renews the world. But the rain couldn't renew what was happening in Da Nang. It couldn't change the appearance of the place, only put a shine on it.

We were met at base operations by an army captain named Jasper. He was one of those people with a broomstick up his ass. If he tried to bend over, he'd break the damn thing. The top of his head looked like a toilet brush. There was a lot of disappointment on his face as we strolled over and introduced ourselves. I guess he expected a bunch of toilet brushes like himself.

We were not army airborne rangers, and he would have to get used to the idea that we would never become rangers. "You men, grab your gear and follow me," was all he said. Mark looked at the rest of us and shrugged his shoulders. When Jasper's back was turned, he flipped him the old chicken.

We all hopped in the back of a pickup truck for a scenic ride around Da Nang. There seemed to be a lot more civilians than usual roaming the streets. Most of them were carrying packs of various shapes and sizes. Some were pushing carts and bicycles piled with what looked like all their possessions.

We arrived at the compound in time to watch the locals fight over the contents of a trash dumpster. There was no such thing as trash as far as these people were concerned; everything could be used for something. Any kind of tin can could be cut apart and used to patch a hole or shingle a shack. A cardboard box was always useful. If it was large enough, it became someone's home. Lumber or a shipping crate was a prized possession, the start of a mansion. Paper was burned to cook food. There were even lunch bags made of computer printout sheets. Any discarded food was examined closely to see if it was worth eating.

I climbed out of the back of the truck and stood at the gate of the compound with Tom, Steve, and Mark. Jasper went to the guard shack with our papers. We were called over one at a time as our papers were checked. While this mini-interrogation was going on, I watched a child help what looked like his grandfather to stack the remains of a wooden packing crate in the back of a handcart. I'm sure they found it odd that an American would take such an interest in what they were doing, but for some reason, I stood there and stared at them. To me, the old man and the child represented the past and the future of this land. I was going to be sent beyond those gates to learn how the minds of those people worked and then, in some way, they were to be persuaded that the way to true happiness was through self-determination and democracy. They already looked determined to me, but I think food was foremost on their minds, not democracy.

I didn't feel needed there, or wanted, for that matter. No matter how important the government thought my assignment was, they couldn't convince me. I wish they had asked the old man and the little boy before they sent me here to help them improve their lives.

The compound where we were to spend the next two weeks consisted of six mobile classrooms, white metal double-wide trailers. It looked more like a trailer court than a school. The grass was neatly trimmed, and flowers grew in boxes at the corners of each trailer. It was quite a contrast from the rest of the base. Grass and flowers were rare, as was the color white.

Jasper showed us around, opening the doors to the classrooms and giving a brief description of what took place in each. We didn't catch what he was talking about most of the time. He was one of those guys who tried to impress everyone with military abbreviations. Every once in a while, he would throw in a little local slang just to confuse things even more. It got to the point where I wanted to grab him and say, "Speak fuckin' English!" But I just smiled and shrugged. Jasper was an asshole.

After the tour, Jasper invited us inside one of the trailers for our "in briefing." We sat around a table while he talked and handed out papers and booklets that explained what he was already trying to explain. It seemed like he didn't want to leave anything to chance, like he thought maybe one of us couldn't read or understand something printed at a third-grade level. This is for the same people who were going to spend an indefinite period of time in Cambodia, surviving by thinking for ourselves.

The school's main purpose was to teach us the history and customs of the people of Southeast Asia. It was going to be interesting to see how they would cover three thousand years of history in two weeks.

Southeast Asia, the first time I saw it, was mostly green—dark green, light green, and green with yellow tints. And where it wasn't green, there was dirt—red, yellow, brown. There were jungle-covered mountains and large bare mountains. Huge rocks jutted out of nowhere, surrounded by green plains. It looked like two giants had had a rock fight in a huge field. Mother Nature had done some of her best work in this land. There was a balance of beauty, and you didn't have to be an artist to see it. You could feel it, smell it, and touch it. Tall, thin palm trees danced slowly in the wind to unheard melodies, and banana trees rattled as they seemed to grow before the eye. There were rubber trees and teak, and bamboo filled in the places where nothing else would grow.

There was grace in the way the clouds moved over the land. They came in low, soft, and billowy, moving toward the mountains, small tufts of cotton at first and then large thunderheads, dark and rain-filled—filled with the life of the land. They were the promise that life would go on, a timeless cycle.

The people were like no others I have ever known, but in some ways, like all the people I have ever known. I tried to find the things that made these people different from myself, but the harder I looked, the more similarities I found. The differences seemed unimportant. They drank weak tea, ate parts of animals that I would have thrown away, looked and dressed differently, and lived in strange homes, but they smiled when I smiled, and we both hated what was happening in their land. They dreamed of the day when rice once again would grow in their fields, children could return to school, and the old people could enjoy the peace of old age. I dreamed of fulfilling their dreams.

The first day of our school was a long pep talk. We got the standard briefing, the one that was supposed to convince us that we were on some kind of holy mission. Knights crusading against the godless hordes of Communism. God and history would judge us heroes who went about the earth improving the lives of all humanity. I don't think any of us believed what was being said. It was just standard government policy, a page in a manual. Something some jerk in Washington dreamed up to justify his job.

As the day dragged on, it got to be a joke. Even the instructor found it hard to keep a straight face. We ended the briefing in a beer garden rewriting the manual. I don't think it would have met with government approval. Steve scribbled "Screw You" across the title page.

The second day, we covered Chinese history. The instructor couldn't pronounce most of the words in the manual. About all we got out of his class was that the Chinese had been around a long time and that they had been messing around in Southeast Asia a lot longer than we had.

The following two weeks were much the same as the first two days. We watched films and listened to a never-ending stream of speakers. We learned a lot, but I'm not sure what we learned would help us understand what our mission was supposed to accomplish.

If anything, we walked away with a feeling of helplessness. We were more sure than ever that what we were doing there would have no beneficial effect on the people or their way of life. It was hard for me to accept, but I grew to believe that there was no solution to the problem in Southeast Asia, at least not one that could be outlined on paper. It's the kind of history that defies logic, that can't be captured on film or written in books, but is lived everyday in the lives of the people. The kind even they can't explain, yet that controls their lives. It reminded me of the time I watched several hundred ants trying to carry a dead grasshopper up a wall. The ants would make it only a few inches before the grasshopper fell back to the ground. They never tried anything different; they just grabbed hold of the dead insect and tried again and again. The old story about how the ants finally made it isn't true. One by one the ants died, and the grasshopper still lay on the ground.

We were the ants and Vietnam was the grasshopper. There had been Chinese ants and French ants, and now there were American ants all with some unexplainable drive to drag Vietnam up and over the wall. No one seemed to know how high the wall was or what was on the other side, if and when they got to the top. I was one of the ants, and I didn't like it.

While we were in school, the State Department had decided to send us to Phnom Penh. The government had made some kind of deal with the Cambodians, to sell them several different types of aircraft. We were to be part of the crew sent to teach local officials how to maintain their new hardware.

Air power was the real power in this part of the world—at

least that is the selling point Uncle Sam used. It wasn't hard to convince the local government. This gift horse was a can't-lose proposition. The United States told them that they really should have all this modern stuff if they wanted to enter the modern world and then gave them the money to buy the stuff. Waiting in the wings were a whole slew of salesmen representing every "Fortune 500" company, with briefcases full of order forms. The locals just sat back and smiled. What they didn't know was that they were talking to the gift-giver at the front door while the thief was sneaking in the back. Uncle Sam was an expert con man.

A lot can be learned about a country and its people by watching what comes and goes through its ports and air terminals, such as who is sending what where and to whom. Everything from new shoes to new bombs usually passes through. It was not always the finished product, but we all knew that it takes leather to make new shoes and that certain explosives make bombs.

Phnom Penh, Cambodia—late October 1967

We bounced off the airplane at Phnom Penh Airport right into the waiting arms of Johnny. Johnny was a round, short Cambodian, whose real name was a mile long and could be pronounced by Americans only if they had speech impediments. So he became known as Johnny, the guy with the beat-up Toyota. Johnny had a big smile, the kind of smile that makes you want to keep one hand in your back pocket. He grinned, "I'm here to be your guide and interpreter. Want to go to hotel now? Okay?"

We loaded all our luggage in, around, and on top of the old red car. We tried to convince Johnny that two trips to the hotel were necessary, but he assured us that everything and everyone would fit. He didn't fool me; I was sure that that wreck was good for only one more trip before it gave up the ghost.

Phnom Penh was an ancient city, dated by temples in varying stages of decay. Everyone seemed to be selling something, from crude carts to stereo equipment. Street vendors filled the air with the smells of local food. As is common throughout Southeast Asia, horns took the place of traffic laws. Anyone who lost his horn was a dead SOB. We arrived at the hotel in one piece, no thanks to Johnny's driving ability. I never did decide whether he was a very good driver or a very bad one.

The hotel was breathtaking, that is, its open sewers took my breath away. I believe the flies made their living taking turns being doorman. The sound of the nearby trains would keep the street noises from keeping guests awake at night. Johnny jumped out of the car, opened the door, and a resounding, "NO, NO, NO!" came from the back seat. Not only was the hotel a shit-hole, but we couldn't stand the thought of Johnny laughing hysterically once he had dumped our luggage and was a block away. We insisted on going first class—or at least second class. After a little more conversation, Johnny finally figured out that he wasn't dealing with a bunch of tenderfeet, and we ended up at a respectable hotel in a civilized part of town.

At six the next morning there was a knock at the door, and there was Johnny, with that same grin on his face, asking, "Ready go work?"

He delivered us to an out-of-the-way, rusty hangar in the northeast corner of the airport. It wasn't what we had expected. You don't work on state-of-the-art aircraft in rusty hangars. Not a soul could be found, so we checked the place out ourselves. There had been no attempt to lock the doors, and many of the windows were without glass. We had to assume that whoever was in charge wasn't concerned about things being stolen. Mark opened a door in the corner of the hangar, and the hollow creaking sound echoing from within confirmed our suspicions; the hangar was empty.

"I've heard of starting from scratch, but this is ridiculous," Steve said as he wiped cobwebs from his face. "We're going to have to find new homes for all the birds and snakes before we can move in here."

Mark asked Johnny, "Who's in charge of this place?"

"He be here in little while," Johnny said, looking off in the direction from which he figured "he" would come. "He come real soon."

Steve and I decided to explore what was to be our base of operations. We decided a lean-to on the south side had the best prospects of being turned into some sort of living space. Perhaps there would be a nail in the wall where we could hang our "Home Sweet Home" sign. We walked through the double doors that separated our future home from the rest of the hangar. In the dim light, we could see a line of workbenches along the outside wall. I finally found a light switch and, much to my surprise, when I flicked it, a blinding light filled the room.

I said, "Love the colors. I always wanted to live in a place with peeling pink walls, and the brown tile sort of hides the dust."

Steve was looking around smiling as he listened to my assessment of the situation. "With a fire hose and a couple weeks' work, we might get through the first layer of dirt," he said, as he ran his hand over the top of the workbenches. At the far end of the room, another door caught our eyes. We looked at each other. "I hope that's a john."

"Me too," I said, as we walked toward the door. When we got close enough, we could tell from the dripping sound that we were right. I turned on the light, and before me appeared an honest-to-god bathroom, with a shower and everything. Well, almost everything—there was a sink, but no toilet.

"Shit! A goddamn bombsite!" Steve was looking at the elevated platform in the far corner. Usually Southeast Asians just use a hole in the floor and throw a pan of water down it when they are done. It takes a little practice before westerners can use one without making a mess of themselves and the room.

"Oh well, it's better than having weeds tickling your butt," Steve agreed as we turned out the light and headed for unexplored territory.

When we walked back out into the hangar, Tom called us to the front door. A cruddy old dark green Chevy was pulling up. There was funny-looking writing on the door. I imagine it said, "Cambodian Army, Official Use Only," just like American staff cars. As the car came to a stop, a gnomelike man with shiny black hair climbed out of the back seat. He was dressed in the khaki uniform of a Cambodian army officer. Walking with a limp, he came over to where we were standing and said, "Welcome to Cambodia, gentlemen. I hope you will find it a pleasant place."

I looked at Steve and whispered, "I guess he doesn't know we've been up to our asses in his country before." Steve just kept smiling in the direction of the officer.

"I'm Major Thu. I will be your liaison officer. If there is anything you need or any information I can help you with, please call on me." The man spoke impeccable English.

Mark thanked the major. Then, out of curiosity, he asked, "Excuse me, Major, I was wondering, have you ever been to the States?"

The major came to attention and replied: "I went to the University of Colorado, Class of '57. Before that, I lived with my parents in Denver. In fact, I spent most of my childhood living all over the country. My father was a Cambodian diplomat. That's how I got into the army." I didn't expect someone to be quite that frank about it; he seemed proud of the fact that his family was in a position of influence.

"There will be a couple of trucks along later this morning," he continued. "They should have enough supplies to make this place more livable. We have also contracted with a local company to repair anything you find wrong with the hangar. They will also be available to assist you in making any modifications you find necessary to accommodate the aircraft."

Mark asked when the aircraft were supposed to arrive, a question that was on all our minds. It was going to take some time before we could turn this rusty shed into a place where we could work on airplanes. The major said the arrival date had not been confirmed. As always, red tape was still holding things up. Mark also asked if we would be restricted to certain areas of the airport since we seemed so far removed from the rest of the facilities. The major assured us that we could use whatever resources the airport had available. Mark thanked the little man and walked him to his car. They talked for a few minutes and then the major drove off.

Mark came walking back looking very pleased. He was chewing one of the major's smelly cigars.

"We're in!"

"What do you mean, 'we're in'?" asked Steve.

Mark just smiled and walked through the big hangar doors and started looking at the ceiling. "The major thinks he's finally hit the big time. He's going to bust his ass to make sure we stay happy." We all followed Mark into the hangar, waiting for him to feed us all the information. It was about time something started going our way.

"The major said he wanted to cooperate with us in every way possible. If there's anything we need, we just have to contact him. He's authorized, from very high up in the government, to see that we get it. I don't think there will be too many people asking questions about what we do around here as long as we keep dear old Major Thu happy—if you know what I mean." What Mark meant was that as long as the major got his cut out of the operation, he didn't care what happened. He could carry on a little black market action with the locals who were going to be working with us. They were always good for smuggling cigarettes downtown, and anything else that the major thought he could find a market for. There was also an understanding that all payrolls were to be doctored. When we hired workers, we would pay them twenty-five cents an hour, but the payroll records that were turned in to the government would show that they were getting fifty cents. The extra twenty-five cents would go to the major. None of the workers would ever complain. They knew if they did, they would never complain again.

There was the sound of squeaking brakes outside. Three large dump trucks full of men and women started unloading. Mark called Johnny, who appeared out of a corner rubbing his eyes. With a yawn, he asked what Mark wanted. Mark pointed toward the mass of people standing in the hangar door. "It's time for you to start earning your paycheck."

Johnny looked at the newcomers and then back at Mark. "What you want me to do with them?"

"Find out who's in charge of the bunch and get them started cleaning this place up. That should take them a couple of days. In the meantime, I'll figure out some kind of procedure on what we will do next."

Johnny went over and talked to the group. He ended up speaking with an older man who seemed to be in charge. He started pointing around to different parts of the hangar. Johnny shook his head up and down and back and forth. Finally, he returned to where we were standing. With a sheepish grin on his face, he walked over to Mark. "What are they supposed to use, sir?"

"What do you mean?"

"What are they supposed to use to clean this place up? There aren't any brooms or mops or anything like that. They want to know what they should use."

Mark looked stunned. He hadn't thought of that. The sheepish look went from Johnny's face to Mark's as he looked at the people waiting for an answer. "I'll get something," he said.

"In what?" Johnny asked. "*We* don't have a truck."

Mark look dumbfounded. "Shit! I'm really off to a good start here. I'm standing here with my thumb up my ass and those people know it. I'm a real smart American."

Johnny suggested that Mark and he go talk to the old man to see if he could help. After a few minutes, they left with him in one of the trucks. The rest of the people started pulling weeds and looking around. Two ladies unloaded a couple of sacks from the back of a truck and started building a fire outside the front doors.

Steve, Tom, and I walked around smiling at the people at work. They smiled back, but no one spoke. We finally got tired of smiling and retreated to a small office in the rear of the building. We each picked out a corner and sat down to relax. I looked around the room. "If someone had told me a year ago that I would be squatting in a dirty office in an aircraft hangar in Cambodia, I would have told them that they had been drinking too damn much. How the hell did I ever get in this place? Two years ago, I was just out of high school and I'd never even *heard* of Cambodia."

Tom and Steve were both sitting with their heads between their legs. Steve said, "Do you ever sit with your eyes closed and think if you hold them closed tight enough, all this will go away? If you think hard enough, somehow you can transport yourself back to the real world?"

Tom said, "Yeah, but the thing that gets to me the worst is when I dream of being back home, of being with my brothers and sisters and my folks. But what really gets me is my girl. I dream about my girl, but all we ever do is talk. That ain't normal. Before I came to this shit-hole, we used to talk a lot, but we used to make love a lot more. I haven't had one goddamn dream about making love to my lady and that ain't right, at least not for me. It really pisses me off. Sometimes, I wonder if it ain't some kind of omen.

"One night, I dreamed about her and she was hiding behind a wall. She wouldn't let me see her. I kept asking her why she was behind that wall and she kept saying, 'Because I love you.' I got mad and woke up." Tom looked up with tears in his eyes. "You know, I couldn't remember what she looked like. I couldn't remember her face!"

Steve and I knew what Tom meant. We'd had dreams like his. Fear draws a line in the mind that good dreams can't cross. It lets you remember just enough of the past to keep you from going nuts.

We didn't try to reassure Tom that everything would be all right. We weren't sure that it *would* be. All we could tell him was that we understood.

Steve got up and walked over to the door and looked out into the hangar. "You know something? I'm going to be a daddy. Kay told me the last time we were in Bangkok. I'm going to be somebody's old man. I know I'm Bong's stepdad, but this time, I'm going to be a *real* father. Tell me, how am I supposed to feel? I think I'm supposed to be happy or something, but I'm not. When Kay told me, the only thing that passed through my mind was, 'I really fucked up this time.' Kay never knew what I was thinking. I caught myself before she could tell how I really felt. I told her I was real tickled and hugged and kissed her.

"I get pissed everytime I think about her having a baby. I'm not mad at her or the fact that she's pregnant. I'm mad because I don't have the faintest idea about how to be a father, and the timing is all wrong. You know, my parents don't even know I'm married. I don't know how they're going to feel when they find out that I married a Thai. I never even thought about it until one day, Kay started asking me what New York was like. Then it hit me—someday I'm going back there. I knew all the time that eventually I'd be going home, but I just didn't think about it that hard. It was like I didn't want to think too hard or want it too much because if I did, maybe then something would happen and I would never make it. Does that make sense to you guys?"

"When Kay came along and we fell in love, it was like something in the back of my mind decided to make as much of a life as I could right here. We got married and everything seemed so fine. We were happy. We *are* happy. When she told me that she was going to have a baby, all of a sudden, it came to me. Someday these two worlds are going to meet. I don't know what's going to happen. It was funny, I was lying in bed thinking about my kid. He's going to be Thai, Russian, American, and Polish. The little fucker is a TRAP. I lay there and laughed my ass off.

"Guess when I get home, I'll just walk up to the front door and say, 'Mom, Dad, meet the little woman. Oh, the kids, they're mine, too. Got anything to eat?' Maybe enough of the old country has worn off that they won't care. One good thing, Kay's Catholic. I'd really be up shit creek if she were Buddhist. I'd go broke trying to buy enough candles to burn. Kay would be praying for my mother's soul and Mom would be praying for Kay's. Hell, I might as well laugh about it, I'm sure not going to cry."

But when Steve turned around and looked at Tom and me, he wasn't laughing. No one said anything for a few minutes, we just looked at each other. It amazed me how people in the same situation often have the same fears, how three people from different backgrounds could share so many of the same feelings. I never have been able to answer the question, Were we this way before the war brought us together, or was it the war that changed our thinking? There was another question on my mind. If we could be so different, yet be so much the same, then how much different were we from the people out in the hangar?

"I'm going to be a father too," I revealed, "My wife's having a baby in about three months. I've been thinking about that word *father*. I've even said it out loud over and over again. It didn't make me feel any different. I've tried being happy and I've tried being scared. I've tried to feel all the things a man is supposed to feel when he finds out he's going to be a father. None of them work. Hell, I don't even know what it's like being *married*. Uncle Sam made sure of that when he sent me to this hellhole before I had a chance to find out what it was all about, and now I'm going to be a *father*. It seems like things got turned around backward somehow. I don't know how you handle it, Steve, but sometimes I can put things on hold, sort of like what they do in the movies when they jump from one scene to another, go from one century to another. It kind of mixes things up, but everything comes together in the end and makes sense. That's the only way I can handle it—just hope that everything turns out all right when they flash 'The End' on the screen."

I got up and looked out the window. There were several small groups of locals standing around talking in the shade at the side of the hangar. I couldn't hear what they were saying, but they kept looking in the direction of the runway. I think they were just enjoying the warm afternoon sun, watching the planes take off and land at the main terminal. It was something I liked to do, too. It didn't matter what their destination was, there was always an element of freedom and excitement watching them come and go. In an airplane the world can take on a whole new appearance in a few hours. A person can escape reality. I watched a 707 take off into the afternoon sun and I wished I was on it. I didn't care how far away it was going. All that mattered was that I would be leaving here. When it had disappeared into the clouds, I turned around to see if maybe the world I was in had changed. It hadn't.

Steve and Tom were sitting in their corners just staring into the empty room. It was small and getting smaller by the minute. I said, "Let's get the hell out of this place. I want to see what's down the road. Maybe there's a place where we can get something to eat, or better yet, something to drink."

Tom and Steve agreed. We walked to the field behind the hangar. Small, scrubby bushes dotted the otherwise bare red dirt. It hadn't rained in several days, and already it had turned rock-hard. The road that passed the side of the hangar had a layer of powder-fine red dust, ground by passing trucks. Our feet made small explosions, puffing the dust and covering our boots.

Since the road was heavily traveled, we decided to follow it. After about a mile, the rest of the airport came into view. The checkerboard red and white control tower stood off to the side of four or five white buildings of various sizes. There were several hangars, arranged haphazardly along the flight line. The names of different airlines were painted on them.

"I do believe there's civilization over there," Steve said, looking in the direction of the main airport.

"Let's check it out," Tom suggested.

"No, I don't think we ought to, not yet," Steve responded. "Let's just see where this road goes."

About the time we thought it was safe to walk down the

middle of the road, three large trucks came speeding around the corner. When they got close enough to see who we were, they slowed down. Four locals were riding in the seat, each wearing New York Yankee baseball caps. They stared at us and then drove off.

"We didn't want a ride anyway, you motherfuckers!" Tom yelled, wiping the dust from his face. "Thanks for the goddamn dirt."

Several minutes later the trucks came into view again. They were stopped at the entrance to a fenced area about the size of two football fields. In the middle of this enclosure was a two-story concrete-block building badly in need of paint. Several other trucks were parked at a loading dock. Off to one side was a line of five or six small wooden hooches.

"I don't think we want to get any closer," Steve said.

"Why?" Tom asked.

"Smell that?" Steve's nose was twitching.

"Smell what?" I asked. There was an aroma in the air, but I didn't know what it was. Hell, there were always strange smells over here.

"I think someone is cooking a little hemp over there, and I don't think it's being used for rope," Steve answered, with a laugh.

I was in the dark. "What do you mean?"

"Marijuana, you dumb ass. What we have here is an 'illicit enterprise.' We'd better leave it alone."

We turned around and started back in the direction of the hangar. About halfway back we were almost run down by two trucks coming from the newly discovered enterprise. "I'd like to get my hands on one of those little bastards!" I growled.

When we got back to the hangar, Major Thu was waiting for us, standing in front of the two trucks that had almost run us down. Steve grabbed me by the arm. "Be cool. Let's see what he wants.

Can I help you, Major?" Steve asked.

"I've come for the boxes," the major answered, pointing into the hangar. He was talking about the large crates that had been delivered later in the morning, which contained spare parts and test equipment for the expected aircraft.

"I can't let you have them yet," Steve said. "They haven't been inventoried."

The major was getting mad. "I need boxes now!"

Steve laughed. "How can you need the boxes now? You don't have any planes yet. Our orders are not to turn loose of anything until it's inventoried. That's the way it is, that's the way it's going to be."

"I'll be back first thing in the morning." The major turned, got into his car, and left, followed by the trucks.

Somewhere along the line, the major must have run into Mark. A few minutes after he left, Mark came driving up. "You dumbshits are off to a good start. What did you say to the major to piss him off?"

Steve told Mark what we had seen that afternoon. "That little drug-dealing, black market bastard is going to play the game by the numbers if I have anything to say about it."

Mark agreed. "I knew there was some reason why I didn't like the little fart. I guess we'll have to spend the night in here to make sure this stuff doesn't disappear."

Tom and Mark set off to hunt up supplies for our stay. Steve and I found enough tools to put some bunks together and cleared a path to the bathroom. "It ain't the Ritz," Steve said looking around at what we had done. "But, it's a GREAT BIG ROOM," he yelled. The hangar echoed with his words. Then he flopped down on his bed. "God, I need Kay!"

None of us said anything for a long time. We lay on our beds staring up at the ceiling, watching the shadows grow longer as the sun called it another day.

"When do we get control of *our* lives? I asked. When do *we* get to decide what's in store tomorrow? Or is this what life is all about?" I had a wrench in my hand. I jumped off the bed and sailed the thing through a window toward the back of the hangar. "Let's get on one of those planes over there," I said, pointing in the direction of the terminal across the runway. I picked up a screwdriver and let it sail in the direction of the wrench. Steve said I'd better stop or we would have to do our inventory out back in the morning.

"Fuck it! Something has to fly or I'll let someone fly. I feel betrayed by the whole goddamn world. I guess I've been one of those stupid bastards who believed that the human race was striving to be something better. I always thought that there was a group of people who knew all the answers. When I was a kid, I was always told what would make me a better person. I had all these rules drilled into my head, and here I am now breaking every fuckin' one of them."

Steve sat up on his bed. "We're seeing all the bad right now. There'll come a day when we'll start seeing the good again. It won't come up and hit you in the face like this war has; it'll come in little bits and pieces—one person, one event at a time. But the good will come. Maybe we're lucky, finding all the shit out at a young age. We've found out that there's very little black and white in the world—just shades of gray. Maybe if we are not too screwed up after this is all over, things will fall into place a little better. Hell, I don't know, maybe I'm full of shit. I get like you, but I've got to think things are going to get better. They may throw my ass in the ground someday and put up a stone that says 'He always thought things would get better.' But what else is there to live for?"

Steve had a way of calming me down. I didn't always agree with what he was saying, but the tone in his voice did the trick. I said, "I just feel disjointed. A person is supposed to feel like he has some control, but I feel like I'm in someone else's body. Some guy came along and said to me, 'Here, take over my body for a while. I've got to get away from all this.' And here I am. I don't have the vaguest idea of what's going on, just filling in the best I can. I don't know what I'm doing here. I'm supposed to be a husband, and thanks to Uncle Sam, I don't know how that feels. I'm going to be a father, and I don't know what that is supposed to feel like. All I'm doing is hanging on, hanging on waiting for things to change. Waiting for that guy to return and take back his body."

I was so wrapped up in what I was saying, I didn't notice that Steve was looking at the side door of the hangar. I turned around to see what had caught his attention. In the dim light were three locals dressed in suits, looking around the hangar and pointing to all the boxes and talking among themselves.

"Can we help you?" Steve said as he walked toward them. The three backed out the door and retreated. Steve and I reached the door just in time to see them drive away in a large car. We didn't understand much of what they were saying, but what little we did catch coupled with the tone of their voices made us believe they weren't too happy that we were there.

"What the hell? I guess that wasn't the welcome wagon. We should have known—they didn't have one of those nice gift baskets."

Steve laughed, "I guess you're right."

We walked back to our beds. "I wonder what those guys were doing on this side of the airport," I said. "Maybe they have business with that warehouse down the road. They were headed in that direction. There's something funny about that place. I can't put my finger on it yet, but something just isn't right."

Steve agreed. Something didn't add up. We all had the same feeling that afternoon. We wanted to keep a safe distance from that warehouse, but we didn't really know why. We were afraid that before we left this place we would find out, and that we couldn't like it.

Tom and Mark returned. They'd scored real well. In fact, they had gotten a lot more than they had originally planned. They not only had clean clothes for us, but they'd also stripped the beds at the hotel of their sheets, blankets, and pillows. The hotel bathrooms also had to be bare because there was a box full of soap and towels.

Tom started removing the towels from the box. "Had to have something to keep the beer cold," he said as he unrolled one of the towels and exposed the large liter bottles of the local brew. "Pain killer!" That evening I was going to need something to numb the pain, to numb my brain.

Mark returned to his truck and came walking back with another boxful of food. "You think this will hold us for the next few hours?" For a few greenbacks, the hotel chef had hustled up some hamburgers and french fries—not an easy task in this part of the world. He had also managed to locate a bunch of canned goods with American labels.

"We're going to eat good if nothing else," Mark said as he placed the box on the floor between the beds. "If we can't go to the hotel, we'll bring the hotel to us."

Steve started telling Mark about our three intruders. Mark decided that it would be a good idea if one of us stayed awake, just in case our friends decided to return. When you are the only foreigners in a different country, you become a little paranoid. Trust is pretty much removed from your vocabulary, at least until it's earned, which is hard to do.

When we had finished eating and the last of the beer was gone, everyone decided that it had been a long day and hit the sack. I volunteered to take the watch. I liked the night. It was a time when I could be alone, a time when I could catch my breath, both physically and mentally. I liked to walk. It didn't matter if I covered very much ground. Sometimes I even walked in circles, but the act of walking seemed to drain all the poison out of my body and to clear my head.

I was more restless than normal that night and didn't think I could sleep. I have always found it hard to sleep in strange places, and this was one strange place. I walked around the hangar for a while, inside and out, finally ending up in Mark's truck half-listening to the radio. In the distance, the blue lights of the taxiways gave a pale, blue tint to the sky. The groan of far-off ground power equipment was familiar and calming. The lights and sounds were a common thread that helped hold my world together.

I was sitting in the truck thinking about nothing, when I felt a hand on my shoulder. I jumped so high my head hit the top of the truck. Before I knew what was happening, I had my revolver cocked and pressed between Johnny's eyes. We both tumbled backward. A deafening blast filled the air as we hit the ground. My left ear was ringing from Johnny's screams and my right ear from the muzzle blast.

I was too scared to move. The two of us lay there on the ground hugging each other.

"Johnny, are you all right?"

"Yes, I think so." Johnny laughed. I don't know what he was laughing about, but it was contagious. By the time Mark, Tom, and Steve arrived, Johnny and I were both laughing and rolling around on the ground. "You're sick!" Mark said. "What the hell is going on out here?"

It wasn't until I started explaining to Mark what had happened that I started shaking. By the time I was done, I could hardly speak. I was scared and angry. I cocked the revolver, pointed it in the air, and kept pulling the trigger until it was empty. There were still echoes ringing in the air as I handed the gun to Mark. "I don't want this thing anymore." Mark reached out and took it from my hand without saying a word.

I walked inside the hangar and leaned against the door. My knees were too weak to support my weight. I didn't try to fight it. As my legs gave way, I slid down the door until I was sitting on the floor. I placed my hand over my eyes and took a deep breath.

"Hey man, I'm okay. See, no holes." I took my hands away from my eyes and looked up at Johnny. There he was with his big smile, holding his shirt open to show me that there were no holes in it.

"I shouldn't sneak up on you," he said as he slid down beside me. "I no do that again!"

I reached over and put my arm around Johnny. "I no do that again either."

That night, Johnny became one of us. Mark, Tom, and Steve came into the hangar and sat down on the floor with Johnny and me. No one talked about what had happened. We joked and made fun of each other, like a bunch of kids, sitting in a circle and talking until the sun came through the crack in the door.

"Baseball caps, damn baseball caps!" shouted Steve. Goddamn baseball caps!" Everyone looked at him.

"What the hell are you talking about?" I asked.

"Those guys yesterday were wearing baseball caps, Yankee baseball caps. Nobody here wears ball caps, at least not all Yankee ball caps. Where did they get them? They looked like a goddamn team."

Steve was right. It wasn't unusual to see different kinds of caps on these people. There were army caps, straw hats, and every once in a while, you would see an American ball cap. But it was rare to see that many caps, all alike, on a group of people. It was particularly unusual to see such new caps. Most were crumpled and dirty and would be worn until there wasn't anything left.

Mark said, "This is an airport. All kinds of things come through this place, probably even baseball caps. Those guys must have broken into a shipment or traded someone for them." He could have been right. But something still didn't sit right about that bunch and we all knew it.

The squeaking of truck brakes interrupted our train of thought. The workers were arriving from town. We hoped they would be more productive than the day before.

There was an obvious difference in the second day's work crew—the children had come with their parents. I looked around and spotted a smile on every face. They felt the same way I did. Kids added something special to everyone's life.

It wasn't long before the smell of cooking food drifted into the hangar, along with the smoke. Halfway through the morning, everything came to a standstill. It was time for breakfast.

Johnny walked over to me. "You come too. Go get other guys. Time to eat." I thanked him, but assured him that we had plenty to eat. "No! No! You come, be mad if you don't." I finally agreed. I had no idea what we were in for, but we were going to find out.

When I told Mark, Tom, and Steve that breakfast was ready, they looked at me. "I didn't know you were cooking," Mark said.

I smiled, "I'm not." I pointed to the smoke coming through the hangar doors. "Out front."

The three of them started walking away. "I'm not up for no raw fish this time of morning." Steve said.

Tom piped in, "Fish, hell, dog or monkey balls. I'm not eating any of that shit!"

I shrugged my shoulders and looked at Mark. "They kind of insist."

Mark shrugged his shoulders back. "What the hell, we've eaten worse." Over Tom and Steve's protests, he said, "Let's go."

Each one of us picked a circle and squatted down among the workers. Everyone was smiling, and I smiled back. I was afraid I was about to become a victim of a practical joke. The lady doing the cooking handed me a large wooden bowl filled with rice. I took it and looked around at the rest of the people to get some indication of what I was to do with it. No one was eating. They were sitting with their hands cupped under the bowls. So I cupped my hands and joined the wait. It finally occurred to me that if I watched the cook, maybe I would get some idea of what was coming next. I might even get some idea of its contents. I didn't spot anything that wasn't familiar—eggs, cucumbers, and some kind of leafy vegetable like lettuce. I bounced around on my toes, puffed out my chest, and gave a sigh of relief. I was hungry.

I had never been a celebrity, but I became one. The children were fascinated by the strange creatures among them. They touched our hair, rubbed our skin, and pulled our ears. When they talked to us and we answered in English (mixed with a few words of Cambodian), they would look at their elders and laugh. When we reached out to touch one of them, they would jump back, laugh, and return again once the hand had been withdrawn. They brought their bowls among us and we ate breakfast. When it was over, we were friends. They took our hands, and a large chain formed as we walked back into the hangar, a chain with a lot of little links, and four big ones. I couldn't help thinking that these parents knew what they were doing. They knew who their baby sitters would be.

Later Major Thu showed up with a couple of helpers. The rest of the morning was spent opening boxes and crates and taking inventory of their contents. The major signed the required paperwork, shook hands with Mark got in his car, and left. "Well, it's all his now, and when I say that it's 'his,' I get the feeling I'm not too far off base," Mark said, shaking his head as he watched the major drive off.

The local workers were doing a good job transforming the hangar from a rusty shed into a respectable aircraft facility. They were starting to find paint under the layers of dirt. Muffled laughter could be heard coming from the rafters and out of the cobwebbed corners. Using the empty boxes and crates, the children had established a small subdivision in one corner of the hangar. I guess we became the local building inspectors because we had to approve all aspects of their construction. Tom found several boxes of spray paint, and before the afternoon was over, there were some really colorful homes—as well as home owners. When evening came, the parents found that eviction can be difficult. There was a lot of kicking and yelling as the residents were removed from their community. Not until they were convinced that the town would be intact the next morning, did the children agree to leave.

Late in the afternoon, Major Thu returned with a telex. Mark's presence was required in Hong Kong. Several of the private contractors involved in the project needed some questions answered. Mark announced, "Vacation time, help me pack my bags, boys. By the way, which one of you is my aide?"

We wrapped our arms around each other. Steve said, "We all are."

"I don't think they will buy that. Besides, someone has to mind the store."

Tom grinned, "Think they would buy Siamese triplets?"

"I don't think so, but that was a good try. Now, figure

out which one of you is going."

Tom pulled a coin from his pocket. "Odd man goes."

Steve won and he started laughing, "Was there ever any question?"

I smacked him on the back. "We didn't have to flip coins to figure out who was the oddest man around here."

"Sore loser."

Tom and I helped Mark and Steve pack. Mark said, "While we're gone, why don't the two of you do a little snooping around. Get an idea where things are at. Johnny can keep these people busy. From what I've seen, they pretty much know what's going on anyway. Here are the keys to my truck. No dents and no tickets." I assured Mark that we would be good boys, and if we weren't, no one would find out.

Mark and Steve left with the major. Tom and I looked at each other and smiled. We were *in charge!* I threw the pickup keys in the air, "Let's get some beer!"

Tom yelled to Johnny, "Hey man, where can we buy some beer?"

Johnny came running. "No sweat man, I show you!"

The three of us jumped in the truck and took off for the other side of the airport. A dirt road ran around the end of the runway. Then it turned to blacktop and disappeared into the trees beyond the fence that marked the airport boundary. We left it just before the fence and continued on toward the main terminal. On the side of the road, the orange robes of three Buddhist monks stood out like three large flowers in an otherwise brown, sparse landscape. Tom honked the horn and passed them.

Johnny turned around in the seat to get a better look at their faces. "Stop! Stop! That's my brother," he yelled, tapping Tom on the shoulder.

"What do you mean, that's your brother?" I asked, looking back at the three orange robes.

"The short one, he my brother."

Tom stopped the truck, then backed up to the monks.

When we were about fifty feet from them, they headed toward the ditch, running and carrying their begging bowls over their heads.

Johnny shouted out the window, "Tran! Tran!" The short, fat monk stopped and looked at the truck. When he saw Johnny, he started to smile. But there was still a look of mistrust on his face. The other two monks lined up behind Johnny's brother. They looked at Johnny and then at Tran, waiting for some indication of what to do next. They were three orange stairsteps, a tall, skinny guy standing in the rear with a monk a little taller than Tran sandwiched in between.

Tran studied the three of us and finally decided it was safe to approach the truck. I opened the door so that Johnny could get out of the truck, and the two of us stood at the edge of the road waiting for his brother to come closer. Tom came from behind the driver's seat and joined us.

Johnny hugged his brother and then introduced him to us. Tran bowed and in a very soft voice said, "Pleased to meet you." Then he turned to Johnny and started talking in Cambodian. They talked for several minutes. Then Johnny said, "Sorry I take so long. Brother have nothing to eat today."

"Well, tell them to get in the back of the truck and we can take care of that," I said, pounding on the side of the truck. Tran looked at me and shook his head no. "Must walk," he said. I became embarrassed. I wasn't thinking too clearly. You don't ask three religious men to ride around in the back of a pickup. But that wasn't the reason they turned us down. I didn't quite understand, but because of something to do with the time of day and the day of the year, they had to walk. We put some money in their begging bowls, so they could buy food. Tran and his brothers bowed and thanked us. We bowed and shook their hands.

The main part of the airport looked like a small part of the rest of the world had been transported here. It was a wonderful place. There were actually signs we could read. Tom drove slowly so we wouldn't miss anything.

Johnny couldn't figure out what all the excitement was about. "You guys still want beer?"

"Yeah, yeah!" Tom said.

"Then, stop here." Johnny pointed to a parking spot just to the left of the main terminal entrance.

"You wait, give me money."

Tom and I dug in our pockets for enough money to cover the damage. "Get something to eat," I said as I handed him the money. "Something American, if you can get it." Johnny gave me the high sign and walked off down the sidewalk.

Tom and I sat in the truck watching the people walk by. They were a cross-section of the world, with different colors and dress and language. I broke the silence. "I wonder what's going on in the rest of the world?" I had no idea what was happening 'out there.' It seemed like a lifetime since I had seen a newspaper other than *Stars and Stripes*, the military propaganda sheet. "I wonder what's on TV."

"I don't have any idea," Tom said. "Maybe there isn't any anymore."

I felt like we were from outer space, aliens visiting this place but not a part of it. All we could do was watch. "Let's get the hell out of this damn truck and see what's going on around here."

"Let's go!" Tom said. The doors were just about ripped from their hinges as we leapt from the truck. Freedom!

We walked down the sidewalk and even that seemed funny. Concrete sidewalks, clean and hard, didn't match our dusty, scuffed boots. It took a few steps before the small clouds of dust stopped welling up from them. We wiped the remaining dust on our pant legs. A futile attempt was made to tidy the rest of our clothes before we entered the terminal. But there was no way of improving our appearance in such a short time. And besides, that wasn't important—we wanted to be in civilization.

The terminal was crowded. People rushed to catch flights and people sat around waiting to rush to catch a flight. We strolled around the terminal, watching and listening. We didn't say much. We bought a newspaper and a *Time* magazine. The highlight of the adventure was watching the TV. We couldn't understand what was being said, but the picture was nice.

A familiar blue baseball cap darted in front of us as we walked back toward the front door. "Let's see where that little creep is going," Tom said. We followed the guy until he disappeared out a side door. We continued, and before long, the blue cap reappeared among a bunch of shipping crates. It was joined by two others, one of them worn by a man driving a forklift.

Tom and I ducked behind one of the crates. We wanted to study the situation without raising suspicion. We tried to get an idea of what the crates contained. Since we couldn't read the writing, we did the next best thing and looked for one with a loose lid. That wasn't hard to find, as none were banded or nailed tightly. They contained wood carvings, everything from ashtrays to bookends. One of the big sellers must have been a statue of a little man with his head up his ass, as there was one full crate of them. Intrigued by the fact that he reminded us of a lot of people we knew, Tom and I each took one.

We had just about decided that we'd seen enough when I noticed something surprising and tapped Tom on the shoulder. "Look over there," I said and pointed to a fenced-in area next to the terminal. "Isn't that our major's shitty old Chevy?"

Tom took a look, "Yep."

"And isn't that the limo that was out at the hangar the other night?"

"Yep."

"Think we ought to stick around and see if there is any connection?"

"Nope. Johnny's going to think we skipped the country if we don't get back. Besides, I'm dry and hungry." Tom had no sense of adventure; at least not when he was hungry.

Johnny was waiting for us when we got back to the truck. "Where you been? Food get cold. You like cold rice?"

"No, I don't like cold rice. Johnny, how well do you know the major?" I asked as I took my share of the food.

"I don't know the major, I don't *want* to know the major."

"What's the matter with the major?"

"You ask someone else. I no want to get in trouble. Major big trouble!"

I frowned, "What do you mean, he's big trouble? I won't tell anyone."

"If the major don't like you, you a dead man. The major is in charge. He the law. People disappear, people the major don't like."

I was getting the chills. "Where do these people go?" I asked.

"Some people die. Some go the major's plantation, work until they die."

The next question, I didn't want to ask. I was afraid of the answer. "Are the people at the hangar the major's people?"

"No! No! They buy jobs from the major."

"What do you mean they buy jobs?" It wasn't unusual to pay a government official for things like that. It was a common practice in that part of the world. I was just hoping it didn't go any further than that.

Johnny explained, "If you owe major money, he sell you job. Then, you pay him back. Sometimes, he buys children until money is paid back."

"That son of a bitch! That's slavery! He's buying and selling people. He owns those people! He owns those kids! They have nothing to say about it!" I was really disgusted. I knew that slavery still existed in some parts of the world, and I had heard rumors that it was even practiced by some tribes in the mountains of Southeast Asia. But I hadn't expected to find it in Phnom Penh!

Johnny couldn't understand why I was mad. "They are happy. They have places to live, plenty to eat. Not a bad life." I don't think I could have made him understand. We had totally different concepts of life. To him, staying alive was the primary mission. Freedom and democracy were secondary, to be worried about once people got beyond the survival stage.

I remember my father telling stories of the old coal mining days, when men went to the mines and worked off the previous week's food bill. Miners were required to live in company houses and buy their supplies in the company store. They often ended up owing the company more than they made. Miners never made enough to escape the system. They were, in fact, slaves to the company. It was a detested way of life, and their main goal was to get out. Through unions and laws, they did a while ago. I'd never expected to encounter such things in my lifetime.

All the time I was going to school, we were taught about the world, everything from a Western viewpoint, of course. The United States was the center of the universe, and the rest of the world revolved around what we did and said. Anyone who didn't believe the way we believed was wrong, or at the least, hadn't achieved our level of enlightenment. And anyone who wasn't a Christian was most likely an evil savage. From reading on my own, I learned that there was a great deal of difference between what was being taught and what was the truth. I couldn't help but think that the truth served me much better in this situation. I was concerned and I cared. If I had listened to the system, I would only care when it interrupted my soap opera.

It was almost dark by the time we returned to the hangar. We had never seen the place with no lights in the windows. It looked larger and more depressing than normal, very cold and forbidding. There were no sounds except for the squeaking and creaking of the tin in the evening breeze.

All the workers had left. The children were gone. I never realized how much they added to the place until they were not there. My ears strained, hoping that maybe some of the people had remained behind waiting for our return. But there was only the sound of the tin.

After the events of the past afternoon, I didn't want to go inside. I really didn't want to think about all that Johnny had told me. I just wanted to relax and enjoy the evening.

The three of us got out of the pickup and walked slowly to the front of the hangar. I could tell by the way Tom and Johnny were acting that they were having the same feelings as I. They were looking the place over very carefully, not really knowing why.

We walked through the door to where the light box was located, and Tom threw the switch. The light was blinding. We squinted and looked the place over. It was brighter than normal. When our eyes grew accustomed to it, we could see that half of the ceiling had been painted white and the whole north wall was a bright blue. The colors had taken away the harshness. It seemed softer, cleaner, and more civilized, a surprising and pleasant contrast to the forbidding outside.

The place was neat and tidy. The floor had been swept, the windows washed, and the cobwebs removed. Even the odor of the paint was pleasant. It seemed like gremlins had been at work while we were gone, and I almost expected to hear laughter coming from the dark corners or to see them scurrying to hide. For a moment, my eyes lingered on the children's boxes in the corner, as they seemed a likely place for gremlins to go. But the boxes were as empty as the rest of the place. I had to smile because they were painted white and blue to match the rest of the hangar, and on several of them were painted names and other signs that I couldn't read. One of them probably read, "No girls allowed!"

Our beds were missing from the center of the floor, so we decided to see what other surprises were waiting for us. As we approached the doors that led from the hangar to the lean-to, we could smell the aroma of food. When the lights were turned on, we found two baked chickens, salads, and bread on the counter. Our beds had been made with fresh linen and turned down. Our clothes had been washed and hung in wall lockers. Freshly shined boots were lined up under each bed. The whole place had been painted, and new tile had been laid on the floor. In the center of the room was a table painted white with four blue chairs tucked in around it, and on the table was a bowl of fruit and flowers with a note. I handed it to Johnny. "What does it say?"

"It says, 'Thank you for the boxes.'"

"These people have really cranked out some work this afternoon," I said. "I can't believe this is the same place. Let's see what they did to the bathroom. I'd like to take a shower before I eat. Looking at all this, I feel dirty."

The bathroom hadn't been painted, but it had been cleaned. Soap was in the shower and clean towels were on the racks. There was still a cracked mirror on the wall, but it shone like a diamond. Someone had placed a cardboard box just inside the door, with a picture of a pair of pants and a shirt drawn on it. I guess it was a Cambodian version of a clothes hamper.

I threw my clothes in the box, turned on the shower, and waited for the steam to start rolling. It never did. Cold showers aren't that bad, I told myself. In fact, after a day like that, it would probably do some good.

"Ain't no hot water," I said as I walked from the bathroom, but I was talking to an empty room. Johnny and Tom were gone. I went to the door and looked out into the hangar, but there was no sign of them. I slipped on a pair of shorts and walked to the front of the hangar. Still no sign of them. I did notice that the truck was gone, so I figured they'd gone to get something.

I lay back on my bed. The sheets were cool and crisp. I propped a pillow under my head and listened to the silence. It wasn't very often that I was alone, and it felt good. I could hear a dog barking in the distance and the night bugs were chirruping and squeaking. A soft breeze was blowing in the window, and I closed my eyes and let it dry the sweat from my face. I liked being alone. It was a time when I could try to sort out things in my mind. But it was as though my head were a file box full of mixed-up three-by-five cards, with some misfiled and others lying around the outside of the box waiting to be added. The longer I put off the task of filing them, the more mixed up they became. Once I was alone, I would pick up each card and read it, have no idea where it fit, lay it down, and go on to the next one. I was always hoping to find one card that gave some indication of where everything was supposed to go, some place where the questions and answers all fit somehow. But the longer I was alone, the more the questions created even more questions, until there was a lump in my throat and anxiety growing inside me as I frantically searched for a card with an answer.

When I was ten years old, our jersey milk cow gave birth to a frisky red calf. We decided to name her Maggie. Her eyes were full of all the fears and questions of new life. Her nose had to smell every new and strange thing in her world. I would watch her jump and run from the most innocent of creatures. She would retreat to her mother's side at the sight of a bug in the grass or a kitten that had wandered from its barn hiding place. Maggie was funny, in her calf-like way, she was learning.

It was my job to feed Maggie from a nipple pail each night and morning. In some respects, I became her mother, and each time I appeared, she would connect me with feeding time. Even when a nipple pail wasn't present, the sight of me would cause her to start running, wagging her tail, rooting at my legs, and trying to suck my fingers. During these times I became aware of what the word instinct *meant. Maggie possessed an element within her that I knew nothing about. Mother Nature had equipped her with most of the answers she would need to survive in her world. Although she didn't always act appropriately, like trying to get milk from my thumb, she was born with the knowledge that milk came from an object that looked like that.*

One afternoon, my father went to the barn early. I looked out my bedroom window and saw him walking across the yard toward the house. He slammed the back door and said to my mother, "The calf is dead in the back stall of the barn."

"Was she all right this morning?" Mother asked.

"As far as I know," Dad responded.

*I came down to the foot of the stairs and looked at my
father. He said, "The calf died."*

*"I know," I answered and walked out the back door. I
didn't want to go to the barn. I didn't want to see Maggie
dead. But I kept walking toward the barn.*

*I stood at the door and looked at the gate to the entrance
of the back stall. Everything seemed so normal. Nothing was
out of place. There were still flies buzzing around, and it still
smelled like a barn. It was the same place I had left early that
morning.*

*When I reached the gate, I took a deep breath and looked
on the other side. There lay Maggie on her side, much the
same as when she was outside soaking up the sun. Her legs
and neck were stretched out, totally relaxed. She didn't look
dead. I picked up her head and looked at her face. There was no
sign of pain or agony in her eyes. Only the limpness of her
neck confirmed my fears. "Why did you die, Maggie?" I asked
as I held her head in my lap. I was looking for an answer, but
of course, I didn't get one. Even if I had, it wouldn't have
made the pain or tears disappear.*

*   *   *

*During my time in the service, a metamorphosis had
been taking place in my mind. All the things that I had held
dear, all the ideas that I used to put my world in proper order
each day were disappearing, dissolving, disintegrating. It
wasn't Vietnam, Cambodia, Laos, or Thailand—it had
nothing to do with Southeast Asia. It wasn't even the war,
although the war perhaps gave birth to my metamorphosis.
The cause came from within me. The world hadn't changed. I
had.*

*I tried to rationalize my changes by attributing
everything to growing up—the casting off of youthful
fantasies and assuming the cold reality of adulthood. But there
was still a void to be filled. There were pieces of the puzzle that
didn't fit. I tried to draw from my reservoir of knowledge and*

experiences, but there were blanks. As I lay on my bed that night, one thought kept running through my mind: The world is a bullshit place. Men had been killing each other for one reason or another since the beginning of time. And someone always found a way to justify it. Our own country's history is broken into eras, the years before and after wars. In the past two hundred years, we have fought four major ones and filled in the time between with a great many little ones. We have annihilated one race of people and enslaved another. Wars have ripped our country apart, and wars have held it together. We have hanged many a man, never taking into account the good he may have done. For his acts of greed, passion, or despair, we have tagged him with label of criminal and ended his life. We have raised generations of young men, sent them off to some foreign place, and asked them to do the things we hang people for at home. It's wrong!

As Doc used to say, "Truth is truth and man has no control over it. It existed before man and it will exist after him. Some have referred to it as God while others prefer to call it physics. But it doesn't matter what truth is called, it's the stuff that holds all things together. You will feel when people don't think you feel, you will love when people don't think you love and you will care when no one thinks you care. You will understand when the rest of the world is confused because you have gone beyond the nature of man in search for your answers. But most of all, you will live life a lonely man because very few will understand. People wrap their lives around them like a blanket protecting themselves from the cold reality, from the truth. They listen, but they do not hear. They are blind. All the senses are in the mind and their minds are tightly wrapped within a blanket."

I thought about what Doc had said. He was a lonely man, an observer who stood off to the side and watched the world go by. He was an old man at twenty-eight, and I sometimes wondered if the way he acted was born from wisdom or despair.

One afternoon, I had found Doc sitting next to the mess hall by himself, soaking up the sun. I walked over to him. "What's going on?" I asked.

Doc closed his eyes, "Tarjan."

I stared at Doc for a moment. "What the hell is a Tarjan?"

"Not what, who," Doc responded. "Tarjan was a Roman king about two thousand years ago. He was probably the most important man in the world at that time."

"Never heard of him," I said.

"He was a king, philosopher, general, reformer. Yep, the most goddamn important man in the world," Doc replied.

"So what?" I asked.

"Tarjan had these two troops sitting up against a mess tent somewhere along the Danube in central Germany. They were talking about some general that no one remembered."

"What's your point?" I asked.

"You see, my boy, everyone wants to believe that he is going to make a difference. Everyone wants to believe that he lives in the most important time in the long history of human existence. Tarjan believed that, Lyndon Johnson believes it, and so does Ho Chi Minh." Doc began to laugh, "Then there's you and me."

I started to laugh along with Doc. "Life is kind of futile, huh?"

"Yep," he said. He stared at me for what seemed a long time. I could see my reflection in his eyes. And then he said, "And fatal."

Sometimes Doc was a dark cloud, and sometimes he was right, and then sometimes he was a dark cloud and right.

Steve came walking through the doors of the leanto holding a chicken in each hand. "Happy Thanksgiving!" he said. He caught me completely by surprise. I had no idea that it was Thanksgiving and in a way, I wished he had forgotten too.

"What are you going to do with those chickens?" I asked as if I didn't know.

"They ain't turkeys, but they'll do. You haven't lived until you've eaten one of my roasted chickens."

"I'm more worried about living *after* I taste one."

Tom and Mark came walking in with sacks full of other kinds of food. They were excited, too.

"Get off your butt and give us a hand. It's Thanksgiving, man!" Tom announced, and shoved me off my bed.

Johnny was standing in the corner with a big smile on his face. I looked at him and he walked over to me. "What's Thanksgiving?" He couldn't grasp the concept. I tried to explain that it was a time to reflect on all the good things that had happened in your life over the past year and also to give thanks for the good fortune received.

"Why you be thankful now, here? I be pissed off. If I were in the States, I be thankful, not here. I be pissed off. Why you be thankful here?"

Johnny was right. I was pissed off and I wasn't one bit thankful. But, I gave him the old standard answer. "I'm alive and I have my health, and someday this will all be over and I'll go back to the States."

Johnny frowned, "I still be pissed off!" He didn't realize that I was trying to hold on to an American family tradition. It had little to do with being thankful. It had much more to do with maintaining a tie to the good parts of my life, the memories, the stability. I wasn't being thankful for the past year, but for all the times before. And I was hoping that many years later, all this would be just a speck in my memories.

Troy, Iowa, was an unincorporated village nestled in the hills of eastern Davis County, with a general store, gas station, and church. There were a few well-kept white houses tucked among the huge shade trees, and coon hounds and cats wandered the streets. Even on a busy day, it was a calm and

*quiet place where people always had time to wave and talk.
In 1955 and 1956, Troy was my home. My father
taught at the high school. We moved into a farmhouse a few
miles north of town with no running water, indoor plumbing,
or central heating. I hated the place! There was no one to play
with and nothing to do. I had to stoop to playing with my
younger brothers and using my imagination. For a city kid,
that was a long and difficult comedown.*

*Now, as I look back, those two years were the happiest of
my life. My family was never poorer—or closer. My brothers
and I had hundreds of acres where we could wander. We were
explorers. Each day brought new, exciting, and undiscovered
places. There were fox dens in the gullies and a raccoon home
in a hollow cottonwood tree. The old barn became an ancient
castle and the outhouse a rocket ship. The frogs, crickets, and
owls told us a story before we went to sleep each night.*

*I believe that my father liked our out-of-the-way farm.
Carrying in the water and cutting firewood was a part of his
childhood. He was more in charge, caring for his family as his
father had.*

*On cold, winter Sunday mornings, my brothers and I
used to crawl into bed with my mother and father. We would
talk and make tents out of the bedclothes. I don't remember
what was said, but I do remember that there was a great deal
of warmth in that cold house.*

*The school was the center of the community, and
everyone gathered there for some activity sooner or later. It
was the center of community pride and community
accomplishments. It was not just a place of learning, but a
place where people cared.*

*An old retired couple lived across the street from the
school. The lady was the school cook, and her husband
collected Indian artifacts. One day the old gentleman came to
the schoolyard with a box of penny suckers and started
handing them out to all the children. His wife came running
out of the school basement scolding, "You'll ruin their*

lunch!" They were *Troy, Iowa.*

Thanksgiving that year was cold, and a gentle snow was falling. My brothers and I spent the morning picking out the best hill for a sleigh ride and waiting for the arrival of our grandparents, aunts, uncles, and cousins. We had all kinds of fun things planned. Anticipation always seems to be the better part of a holiday for children, but in this case, it all came true. In my mind, it was the perfect Thanksgiving, with the snow-covered hills, the food, and the warmth of caring people.

Thanksgiving 1967 was different. Steve cooked the chickens while the rest of us went to the market. When it finally came together, we had a fine feast, although different. During the meal, we exchanged memories of past Thanksgivings. We talked about family traditions and that one bad turkey that had shown up at everyone's house. But, very little was said about the Thanksgiving at hand.

When we were about half done with our meal, Johnny came walking into the room and asked, "Can we have Thanksgiving, too?"

We all turned and looked in his direction. Steve pulled the spare chair out from under the table. "Sure Johnny, dig in."

Johnny hesitated. "No! No!" Then he went to the hangar door. A moment later, a parade of adults and children came streaming in with their arms full of food and huge smiles on their faces. "See, we have Thanksgiving, too!"

I don't know if those people grasped the meaning of the holiday or if they just thought it was a good excuse to eat a lot. I would like to think they did; but it didn't matter. The meaning was there anyway.

Mekong Delta, Vietnam—November 1967

Three days after Thanksgiving, we went down into the delta to retrieve the electronics gear from a downed A-1E. We were to pick up a squad of South Vietnamese (ARVN) troops at Da Nang who would set up a perimeter at the crash site. After the general hassle of getting everything organized and cleared through the proper channels, we boarded three Hueys and left Da Nang.

Mark sat down beside me and said, "We won't have to worry about anyone moving into the A-1E."

I laughed a little. "No, I don't think so."

Mark was referring to a C-123 we had blown up in Laos several months before. We had gotten to the crash site about two weeks after the plane had gone down. By that time, several families had moved into the cargo bay. We had never been faced with this kind of problem before, so Mark radioed back to command, "We've got a bunch of locals calling this wreck home. They've already stripped it of anything of value. All that's left is a bare shell. What do we do?"

"Move out. Blow it up!"

Mark went to the oldest man he could find and tried to explain what was going to happen. But the old gentleman didn't understand. They were mountain tribe people, and they hadn't been exposed to Americans. They must have had a totally different language, because no matter what we tried, they just looked at one another. Finally, Mark said, "Get the charges. We'll see if they understand that." Tom brought Mark the explosives. Mark held them in the air. "BOOM!" Then, he went to the plane. "BOOM!" They understood. The women cried and screamed, and the children ran toward the jungle. Everyone chattered and scuttled around grabbing belongings. An old man held out a basket and shook it at me. I don't know what he said, but hate, fear, and tears were in his eyes.

We blew up the plane. As the choppers left, I looked down on the fire in the clearing. No one came out of the jungle. The people were gone. I turned around, leaned back against the seat, and stared at the jungle ahead. I had never destroyed someone's home before.

The delta was a patchwork quilt, it looked peaceful and clean. Small clumps of trees marked the farmhouses and larger clumps marked the villages. The A-1E had gone down near one of the large clumps. The choppers circled the clump of trees several times and then set down in the rice paddy next to the crashed plane. We unloaded our tools and gear. The ARVN troops did the same. We all stood together and watched the choppers leave.

"Let's get to it." Mark picked up his gear and started walking toward the plane. Tom, Steve, and I followed.

"Where in the hell are those guys going?" Steve asked Mark. The ARVN squad was moving toward the village.

"They're probably going to check things out." Mark said as we moved in and went to work.

I was on the backbone of the plane, just behind the cockpit, when the first blast of automatic weapon fire raked the plane. I heard a "thump thump"; a round had hit the plane on either side of my right leg. I jumped from the aircraft.

"Where in the fuck did that come from?" I landed beside Steve, who was looking toward the village.

"Over there!" He motioned with his head. "Where in the hell are our little buddies?" Steve rolled over on his back and checked his clip.

"Beats me!"

Mark came crawling over. "Where did that come from?"

"Over there," I said.

"I know, but *where* over there?"

Our questions became unimportant. The ARVN squad was crossing the field shouting and shooting their weapons in the air. They were dragging and taking turns beating a young man. When they were halfway to the plane, they threw him down on the ground and each one of them emptied his weapons into the man's body. Then they dragged the limp corpse over to us and dropped it at our feet. The squad leader had a big smile on his face. "VC! VC!" he shouted.

I knocked his helmet off, grabbed him by the hair, and threw him to the ground. With the butt of my revolver, I knocked his front teeth out. I cocked the gun and stuck the barrel in his mouth. "You lowlife son of a bitch!"

The frenzy that filled the next few minutes was a blur. Flashing pain filled my head as I rolled over into the dirt. There were muffled screams in Vietnamese and English. In my semiconscious state, the only thing that came through was someone yelling, "We're not animals!" Then, I passed out.

I don't know what had happened the rest of the afternoon. When I woke up, the ARVN soldiers were gone and Steve, Mark, and Tom were loading our gear into a waiting chopper.

"You ready to go, kid?" Mark held out his hand to help me up.

"What happened?"

"We'll talk about it later." Mark pushed me toward the chopper.

We never did talk about it "later." I knew that I had screwed up. And like a little kid, I hoped if I ignored the situation, everyone else would too. But it wasn't really ignored; it was suppressed, placed in that file cabinet in the dark basement of our minds with a white tag on the front of the drawer titled WE ARE NOT ANIMALS!

Phnom Penh, Cambodia—November 1967

We caught a C-123 out of Saigon the following day and returned to Phnom Penh. It was late in the evening and a gentle rain was starting to fall. The wind was blowing cold for Cambodia in November.

The hangar was dark except for the small lightbulb that burned over the main doors. Huddled in the shadows at the corner of the door was an orange pile that turned out to be

Johnny's brother, Tran, the monk. Mark jumped out of the truck and walked toward Tran. "Can we help you, sir?"

Tran shaded his eyes with his hands and stared in our direction. "Are you the Americans? I'm looking for my brother, Johnny. Have you seen him?"

Mark started to unlock the hangar doors and replied "We've been gone for a couple of days. I figure Johnny is downtown. He'll be around in the morning, if you want to come back then."

Tran lowered his head and backed up a few steps. "I need to find him soon. I have no place to stay. I'm no longer a monk."

"Well, that's a horse of a different color."

Tran gave Mark a puzzled look. Mark started to laugh and opened the door. "I guess I should have said, 'Come on in, you can wait here.'" Tran smiled back and walked into the hangar.

I fumbled in the corner until I found the main light switch. A loud clunk filled the hollow hangar as the lights started buzzing and slowly grew bright. "Home sweet home! Home sweet fuckin' home!" Steve's voice echoed off the walls as he pranced and danced his way across the floor. We all dropped our gear just inside the door and headed to the kitchen.

Tom said, "I'm so mean and hungry, I could eat the doorknobs off a bull. And, I'm so goddamn good, I'll even do the cooking." He took a bow and opened the door to the kitchen. Steve pushed him aside.

"No, thank you, my momma told me never to eat bull doorknobs. I think I'll just settle for a baloney sandwich."

"Well, shoot man, don't you know that's what baloney is made of? They put all kinds of shit in that stuff." Tom shoved Steve. "You're awful picky for a man that gets drunk and wolfs down monkey balls."

"Those aren't really monkey balls."

"Oh, yeah? And I suppose you think you were eating fried chicken, too? Well, I've got news for you. Chickens don't have four feet. And the monkey skins weren't sitting there because they were off taking a shower someplace."

Tran stood and watched Tom and Steve go at one another. It was obvious that he didn't understand what was going on. Tom finally turned to him and asked, "Hey, Tran-monk-sir or whatever you're called, ain't it true you people eat monkeys?"

Tran, looking hurt and sad, answered, "I'm sorry, sir, but I don't eat meat." He looked Tom in the eyes and then turned and started walking to the far side of the hangar.

Tom knew he'd screwed up. "Goddamn man! I'm sorry, I mean . . ."

I grabbed Tom's arm. "Why don't you shut up!"

Tran squatted down against the wall and stared back across the floor at the rest of us. It made me feel uneasy, but that wasn't unusual. Preachers, priests, and now monks always made me feel uneasy. But as I watched Tran, my uneasiness changed to pity, and the pity to concern. I walked across the hangar and asked, "Would you like something to eat?"

"No, thank you. I'll just wait here for Johnny. I'm happy to be in out of the cold."

"How long has it been since you ate? We have plenty, so don't worry that, I mean, we have other things besides meat. You don't have to worry about Tom. He just doesn't know how to act around monks. He's never been around people like you before." Now, I felt like I had messed up, too, and it was time to retreat. "I'll bring you something anyway."

Tran didn't protest, so I went back to the kitchen and found an orange and a couple of apples. It was a long walk back across the floor and I kept asking myself, "What do I say to a monk without putting my foot in my mouth?" Then I thought, "He ain't a monk no more."

"Why did you decide not to be a monk anymore?" The words just popped out of my mouth. That's what I was thinking and I knew that was what everyone else was wondering. I believe Tran knew he would be asked that question if he stayed very long. After all, he was the one who had told us the reason he had come. He didn't have to do that.

Tran took the fruit and then the floodgate opened. "I have always been a monk, and I will always be a monk. I can never stop serving Buddha. He is all I know, He is all I am. My parents took me to the monastery when I was five years old and gave me to the monks. I was raised in the ways of the great Buddha. He was my parent and my teacher. I lived in His house and I ate at His table. I follow the "Eightfold Path" and I learned the Dharma. When the time came for me to leave the temple and wander among men, I carried the word of the great Buddha. I was the word. I had given up myself and the knowledge and want of worldly pleasures. I was the greatest of all teachers. I was an enlightened spirit among men. But only the young and the old would listen, only the young and old wanted to learn. My country is in turmoil and I cannot help it find peace."

I sat down beside Tran and leaned against the wall. "It seems to me you've taken on an awful big job. Maybe it's too big for just one man."

"No no, the great Buddha was just one man. The people listened and respected Him."

And I thought *I* was confused. Poor Tran was completely lost. I said, "There have been many great men, including the great Buddha. Look around. If they were so great, why is the world the way it is today? People may have listened, but they didn't learn, did they?"

"No no! I am not saying that I am as great as Buddha. I can never be as great as the Buddha. If a man is dying from hunger and needs a cup of food and I have food, but only half a cup, the man will eventually die. Each day, I go out into the morning with my begging bowl, and before the noon sun, my bowl is full. It was filled from half-full bowls, half the size of mine. What I am doing is taking the food of a hungry man."

"You know, Tran, I'm sitting here beside you, and you can turn your head and see me. You can follow me tonight and all day tomorrow. You can watch me and ask me what I'm doing, but you won't know me. You'll know about me, but you won't know me. Maybe you assume the man is dying of hunger, maybe you should give him the bowl and see how much he eats."

I don't know if what I said made sense, and if it did, I don't know if I believed it. But, I don't think that was what was important. What *was* important was this man, a man who was trying to do some good in this world.

"Did you ever stop and wonder if the great Buddha knew all that could be known? Maybe he did in his time, but He had to learn it. Maybe you aren't too different from Him. You are learning."

Tran didn't respond; he just sat there with a pensive stare. Before I got up and left Tran with his thoughts, I asked, "One last thing, when is a holy man most needed?" I liked Tran. He was a human holy man with doubts, human doubts like mine.

Johnny came the next morning and took Tran to their village in the mountains. I don't know if Tran is a monk today. I never saw him again, but I remember him, and I think he would like that.

Phnom Penh, Cambodia—December 1967

Mark returned from a meeting with Major Thu late one evening. He threw his briefcase in the corner and flopped down on his bunk.

"That man is a major pain in my ass. The arrogant son of a bitch has no couth. Graft and corruption are a way of life in this country. They don't even *try* to hide it. The man is demanding 'his' aircraft. He's got this idea that Uncle Sam is going to provide him with his own air force. Hell, he might be right. I don't know anymore. He's got a heroin and marijuana factory right down the road. Shit, we've all seen that. He's got warehouses full of guns, TVs, stereos, and who knows what else. And, now, he wants *his* aircraft."

Steve had an easy answer. "Tell the mother to get screwed. Call the embassy in Saigon and tell them about the black market and drugs here."

"I did, and they didn't act surprised. They said they'd get

back to me later. And that was the end of that."

In 1967, I didn't see too many drugs in Southeast Asia. I'm sure they were present, but not to the extent they were later on. I had heard of heroin and marijuana, but they had never had an impact on my life. I knew what the black market was, but I couldn't see that much wrong with it. It sounded like the other-side-of-the-track free enterprise system to me.

"What's the big deal here anyway?" I asked.

Mark gave me the stupid-hick look. "The big deal is, our major is supplying drugs and guns to anyone in Southeast Asia who has the bucks to buy them. Now he wants a few planes so that he can expand his operation. And as near as I can tell, our dear old uncle is willing to let him get away with it."

Steve asked me, "Have you ever smoked a joint? You don't give a shit for nothing. I'll bet there's some GI down in the delta right now puffin' away packin' his M-60. You want him backin' you up? I'll bet you a dollar the weed came from good old Major Thu."

Two days later, Mark got his reply from Saigon: "Pack up. You are being replaced by a civilian airline. Report back to Da Nang." It didn't make sense. We hadn't even gotten started. We didn't really know what our mission was, but we must have hit a nerve someplace. Everything came to an abrupt standstill.

"Does this mean we're fired?" I asked Mark.

"I guess so."

"Well, what do we do with all the stuff in this place?"

"We just lock the doors and give the keys to Major Thu."

"What about Johnny?"

"He works for the major."

"Ah, man, that sucks!"

Johnny had a dream of living in America. That's all he talked about. He had learned English so that he could live in America. He read books and magazines about America and went to movies about Americans. He dressed like an American. And I believe he thought if he associated with Americans enough, sooner or later someone would take him there. The morning he found out we were leaving, he came walking into the hangar and looked at our bags stacked in the doorway.

"Where are you guys going?"

"We're going to Da Nang," Mark told him.

"When you come back?"

"We're not."

The smile faded from Johnny's face. "You no come back?"

"No."

"Maybe other Americans come, yes?"

"Yeah, other Americans are coming."

The smile came back to Johnny's face. His dream was still alive.

I learned to live without my soul.

Da Nang, Vietnam—December 1967

At the end of 1967, just before the Tet offensive, our team was sent up the highway north of Da Nang. A Jolly Green helicopter had gone in a few miles off the highway. We checked a crewcab pickup out at the motor pool, loaded our equipment in the back, and started up the road. The highway was clogged with traffic. Buses and trucks were overflowing with passengers, and people were pushing and pulling two-wheeled carts filled with all their belongings. There were bicycles and motorbikes so loaded down that it was almost impossible to see their riders. Horns were honking and people were chattering, mass confusion. Something was about to happen, but we didn't know what. It seemed to take hours to go a kilometer. Finally, about noon, we reached our turnoff, a narrow asphalt road that left the main highway and wandered through the flatlands toward a long wide valley. It was a spectacular vista. Dark gray clouds hung low between the mountains, and long rays of sunshine streaked the landscape between the clouds. Green was everywhere. The light green of the rice fields changed to a medium green in the foothills and then became the dark green of the mountainsides where they met the clouds. We were following a black ribbon into a serene, green dream.

Steve was the first to notice the strangeness in this place.

"There ain't no people. They all seem to be gone. What do you think is going on?"

Mark was looking out the window of the truck. "I noticed that too, I don't like it." There was an eerie quiet, not even the far-off sounds like airplanes or trucks that had always seemed to be with us.

Tom had turned the radio down soon after we left the base. But Mark decided it might be a good idea to listen and see what was going on. All we could get was static and garbled transmissions, even on the high bands. Mark kept playing with the radio and finally decided that we would have to find some higher ground.

"Take the next road that looks like it heads toward the mountains," he ordered. "There's a lot of traffic on this thing, but I'll be damned if I know what's going on."

We drove on for about another five kilometers until we found a well-traveled path that led into the foothills. At the end of the path was a rusty white iron gate attached to a dirty white wall that disappeared into the jungle about two hundred feet in each direction. The place looked like something the French had built. There was an air of decaying opulence about it. Beyond the wall was a grove of towering palm trees, their tops linked to form a huge umbrella. Beneath the trees, in the center of the compound, was a large white house. It, too, was in a state of decay. Banana plants grew among another six or eight small brown bungalows randomly placed around the big white house.

Mark stepped out of the truck and walked over to the gates. He looked through the bars for several seconds and then returned to the truck.

"Hop out, guys. Lock and load. Let's see if anyone is at home." We opened the gates and walked into the shade of the palm trees. The air was close and hot. The humidity must have been two hundred percent. Our clothes were wet with sweat within seconds. Nothing moved and there wasn't a sound as we headed toward the big house.

Steve whispered to me, "I wonder where all the chickens and pigs are at?"

I half-turned around and whispered back, "Who gives a shit about the chickens and pigs! Where are all the people?"

Mark and Tom went to the front door of the old house. They walked the length of the front porch looking in all the front windows. Then they opened the door and walked in. Steve and I remained outside and watched for any signs of life. After several minutes, Tom and Mark reappeared at the front door. As Mark came down the steps, he pointed over his shoulder. "We got a body at the back door. Looks like he bought it while trying to get away." Then he pointed to the right and looked at Steve and me. "Check those bungalows over there. Tom and I'll check the rest."

Steve and I checked the first two bungalows. Whoever had lived there hadn't been gone too long. The place was clean, and there were fresh bananas on the table, along with several bowls that had the remains of a meal. A basket with some fresh laundry was just inside the door. We went back outside and checked around and under the houses. "Nobody home," Steve said.

As we approached the third bungalow, we could hear flies buzzing, we knew what was inside. My knees grew weak, and a knot started growing in my stomach. I didn't want to go in there. I looked over at Steve. He was rubbing the back of his neck and looking at the front door. We looked at each other, and neither of us said a word; we knew what had to be done. I started up the steps first. When I got to the door, I stopped and waited for Steve. When he got to the top of the steps, we entered the house together.

The place had been ransacked and flies were buzzing all over the place. A broken table was covered with papers and maps, and a broken radio sat on top of the mess. But that wasn't what caught our eyes. Against the back wall were three bodies, slumped in a pile, each with a bullet hole in the back of the head. I went over and nudged them with the barrel of my rifle. They were as stiff as boards. I closed my eyes. All of a sudden, it was too hot in that house, and I knew if I didn't get some air, I was going to lose my lunch. "Let's get the fuck out of here," I told Steve.

When we got back outside, an ARVN squad came marching up in single file. They caught us by surprise. I don't know
where they came from—they just appeared. The squad leader
had a big smile on his face.

"VC!" he said and pointed at the bungalow. Then he raised
his hand and made a circle in the air. "VC all around here. What
you do here?"

I told him about the helicopter and why we had come to
this place.

"No can do, no can do. Have to leave. VC right out there."
He pointed back down at the flatlands. I couldn't see a damn
thing, but I took his word for it.

Mark and Tom walked up. Mark stared at the ARVN
squad and then looked at us. "What did you find?"

"Three dead, over there." I pointed at the bungalow.

"We've got five dead and two alive. There are two kids in
that far hut, scared to death." Mark looked at the squad leader,
and asked, "Are you in charge here?"

"Yes."

"Do you know anything about those kids?"

"No, no. I know nothing about children."

Mark asked Tom, "Would you show the sergeant here
where the kids are?" Mark started walking toward the truck.
"Let's go see if we can get that radio to work."

"I think we've got more to worry about than that radio," I
said. "The sergeant tells us there are VC all over the valley down
there," I said, waving my hand in the direction of the fields.

"Well, we'll need the radio more than ever now, won't
we?"

I hadn't thought about that. "I guess you're right."

"Yep, that's why I get the big bucks."

It seemed like it was taking Tom as awful long time, so
Mark sent Steve to check on him. I sat and played with the radio
until I finally got in contact with operations. Mark was looking
at his maps on the hood of the pickup. I walked around and told
him I had made contact.

"Good. Now maybe we can figure out what our next move's going to be."

Mark radioed in our location and situation. There was a long pause on the other end of the radio.

"Captain, you aren't supposed to be there."

"I know where I'm supposed to be, and I know where I am. What I want to know is how the hell do I get out of here? Intelligence tells me that the sectors east and south of here are overrun with VC. Can you confirm that?"

"Affirmative."

"Well, what's my next move?"

"Are you under attack?"

"No."

"Sit tight, we'll get back to you."

"That's fuckin' great! I should have said yes."

Mark threw the mike into the front seat of the truck. "Will you go see what's taking those guys so damn long?" Mark was getting pissed. I picked up my weapon and started walking to the bungalow where Tom and Steve were supposed to be.

When I got to the house, Tom was sitting on the bottom step that led up to the front porch. Steve was sitting behind Tom, several steps further up. They both were staring straight ahead with blank expressions on their faces.

"What's up, guys?"

They didn't say a word. Their heads and eyes just moved in the direction of the bungalow. Tom turned back and he stared at the ground. And then, in a soft, broken voice, he said, "They killed them."

I knew what was hidden around the corner of the house. As sure as I was alive, I knew what was there. Something inside told me I had to look.

There was a young girl about seven or eight, lying face down in the dirt, her blue dress was pulled up so it partly hid the back of her head. She was barefoot and her feet were heavily calloused. Beside her lay a naked baby, maybe six months old, on its back with arms and legs stretched out, covered with blood.

There was no face. It was obvious that the baby was dead, so I turned to the older girl. I pulled the dress away from her head and saw that the back of her head was flattened. I replaced the dress over her head, turned around, and walked away. Steve, Tom, and I walked back to the truck. No one said a word.

Mark could tell that something was wrong when we walked up. But no one volunteered anything. Tom sat down on the tailgate of the truck. Steve flopped into the back seat. I squatted under a nearby tree.

"Will someone tell me what happened back there?" Mark asked as he looked at each one of us.

Finally, Steve began to talk. "I didn't get in on it. Tom did. But I don't think he's in any condition to give you the answers. As near as I can tell, Tom and the ARVN squad went back to the hut but couldn't find the kids. They weren't inside. Tom looked around and found the older child hiding under the bungalow. When he went under the house, he found the baby, too. He caught the girl and brought her out, and then went back for the baby. He brought the baby out and handed her to one of the ARVN soldiers and went back a third time to gather up their belongings. When he finally emerged from under the hut, the oldest girl was already dead and the ARVN soldier was swinging the baby like a ball bat, bashing its head against the corner of the bungalow. What happened after that, I don't know. When I got there, the ARVN troops were gone and I found Tom standing, looking at the kids. He chattered like a woodpecker for about thirty seconds, but he hasn't said a word since.

Mark walked over to Tom and asked, "Are you going to be all right, guy?"

Tom slowly raised his head and moaned, "I handed him the baby." Then he hung his head again.

Mark didn't say anything else. He knocked a couple of times on the top of Tom's helmet, turned around, and walked away. I didn't know what to do, so I just sat there under the tree and looked out over the countryside. Mark was busy talking on the radio. Finally, he announced, "It seems like we're on our own. If we can get back to the main highway, we'll be all right. The way I've got it figured, if we get out of here now, we can get back before dark. The VC aren't going to make their positions known during daylight. There's not enough cover down there. So, let's get out of here."

I jumped in behind the wheel. Tom and Steve sat in the back. I think they needed the fresh air. Mark sat in the seat next to me. I started the truck and jammed it into gear, smashed the accelerator to the floor, and held it there. I don't remember too much about the trip back to the highway. I wasn't afraid of the VC. At the time, I figured the best thing to do was take my anger out on the truck. There was nothing else I could do.

Tom was never the same again. He stayed drunk day and night, and no one could talk to him. Then he became very quiet and withdrawn. All of a sudden, the whole world had become a sick joke and he didn't give a shit for anything. Finally, one night he freaked out down in Dogpatch, the bar district of Da Nang. The Air Police picked him up, screaming and drinking and pissing in the middle of the street after curfew.

The last time I saw him, he was getting on a plane for the hospital in the Philippines. He had a big smile on his face. "Don't worry about me, boys. I've got my fuckin' ticket home." A couple of years later, I heard that Tom had OD'd on something in a little town in Maine.

Bangkok, Thailand—December 1967

After Tom left, Mark went to Tokyo on R&R, Steve went to Korat to see his family and I went to Bangkok. I took a room at a fancy hotel, locked myself in, and slept for twenty-four hours. The next morning, I hired a cab and rode around all day. The following day, I wandered the streets and back alleys. I couldn't get comfortable. I was an alien with no place to go; no place fit and I was angry. I sat on the patio at the hotel watching my reflection in the sliding glass doors. There I was in a white shirt, with a dark tan, my bottle of Jack Daniels on a glass-topped table, staying in an international city of intrigue. This was supposed to be the stuff that movies are made of—but it was a nightmare.

I lay on my bed one evening reading an article in *Stars and Stripes*. A small town in Ohio was sending all its servicemen Christmas presents to show their gratitude to their boys in Vietnam. I thought, "I'd like to go to that little town. I'd like to load the whole town on an airplane and bring them over here. I'd like to yank some fat bastard away from his recliner and TV set and toss him on the plane. Then I'd find the local ladies club and I'd show them that there were greater problems than the couch clashing with the drapes, or their daughter making out with her latest boyfriend, or junior not making the basketball team. I'd load them all and bring them to Vietnam, and I'd be their travel guide.

"Gather around folks. We have a busy schedule. This is going to be a one-day whirlwind tour of the war. Everyone stick close. We wouldn't want anyone wandering off and getting shot, now would we?

"First on our itinerary is the Napalmed Native Village. The folks there range from rare to well-done. They're a friendly bunch when they're not preoccupied with fire.

"Next, we'll visit a well-known Fire Base. Now if you're lucky, you'll get to see one of your local heroes blown apart by an enemy mortar. Doesn't that sound exciting?

"At noon, we will be eating in one of the country's finest hotels. To add to your dining pleasure, you will be able to experience the 'rush' of a terrorist bomb attack.

"After lunch, we'll visit a negotiation session between the Good Guys and the Bad Guys. That's where you get to see a bunch of statesmen stick their heads in buckets of sand.

"Before we leave, I hope you'll take advantage of our gift and souvenir shop. I understand we have a large selection of

dried human body parts. Specials this week are ears, toes, and
fingers. Please make a note of our Body Grab Bag near the
door. No two are alike, and by the way, the small ones are two
for the price of one.
   "Last, we'll be boarding the plane for the trip home at
4:00 P.M. At this time, on behalf of the president and all the
members of Congress, I wish to thank you for visiting
Vietnam. Many happy dreams."

It seemed like the whole world was marching by and I was
marking time. The newspapers and magazines were full of
everyday life. New cars and TVs were being built. People were
buying new houses and taking vacations. The streets were full
of men and women in new clothes carrying shopping bags full
of more new clothes. Life was going on. I had had this hick
impression that when a country went to war, the people made
sacrifices. But that didn't seem to be the case in this war. The war
was just something that took up five minutes on the six o'clock
news. I guess I was jealous of the folks back home. I had just
tasted the freedom of adulthood when Uncle Sam came along
and sent me to Vietnam. As I sat there in that hotel, I think it was
more than anger I was feeling. Deep down inside, there was also
fear. A fear of the contrasts I was seeing and feeling, of the
extremes existing in the definition of human existence. I had
wanted a new car, a new house, and new clothes. I wanted all the
things that add up to the American dream. But at that time and
place, the dream didn't seem so important. At that moment, I
would have settled for so much less. And yet, I was too young
to settle for less; I was too young to give up.

Da Nang, Vietnam—January 1968

   After Mark returned from R&R, Steve and I met him back
at Da Nang. Christmas and the new year had come and gone,

and my tour was about half over. Steve and Mark were feeling down after their return to reality. The three of us were wondering what our future would be now that Tom was gone. Mark went to operations for our next assignment and was told there was none. We were to sit tight until further notice. "I got a real funny feeling down there," Mark said. "They acted like they didn't want me around, that they were too busy to bother with me."

"I hate this goddamn place," Steve said, "but, it's better than the bush. If you want to know what I really think, I think our brotherhood is being dissolved."

Mark nodded. "I think you're right."

Steve started smiling. "Hell, maybe they will forget about us and we can just hang out down in Dogpatch until it's time to leave."

Steve's dream was not meant to be. On the last day of January 1968, all hell broke loose. The National Liberation Front (NLF) launched a rocket attack against Da Nang. Stuff was blowing up all over the place and it was a madhouse. The NLF caught Uncle Sam with his ass hanging out and was burning it bad.

Steve and I were on our way from the barracks to the mess hall when the rockets started falling. One of them hit the barracks, so we started back to see how much damage was done. About the time we turned around, one of the rockets hit the mess hall. Chunks of concrete and gravel were flying through the air and the sound of broken glass was all around. It seemed like everything was either on fire or blowing up. "Let's find a fuckin' bunker!" I yelled at Steve. Steve didn't argue. We found a pile of sandbags, dove over the side, and landed on a bunch of GIs who had arrived before us. Soon there were people landing on us and the bunker became a mass of twisted arms and legs. I think more people were injured from jumping into bunkers than were hurt by the rockets.

When things calmed down a little, we decided to find Mark. We figured that he was at operations near the flight line.

There was debris covering the streets and hanging over the sidewalks. People were running around yelling and screaming orders and directions. Some crazy major grabbed me by the arm, and asked, "Where's your helmet, Airman?"

"Back at the barracks, sir."

"Well, get your ass back there and get it."

"I can't, sir."

"Why not?"

"There ain't no barracks."

Steve said, with a real serious expression on his face, "Major, he can borrow mine."

"Fine, fine." The dumb bastard was so shook up, he didn't realize what he had just agreed to. Steve and I walked away laughing.

We found Mark standing in front of operations watching the F-4s in the alert cell burn. "It's amazing, those little sons of bitches can pound a pole in the ground, hook a rocket to it, and hit an airplane dead center five miles away. Boom-boom-boom, everyone dead center." We stood there for a few minutes watching the fires and mayhem. "You can't fight technology," he said.

"What are we going to do now?"

"The two of you are to report to the counter inside. The guy behind it was saying something about guard duty," Mark said.

"That's just fuckin' great," I said. "Can't you get us out of it? We don't know what's going on around here."

"From the looks of things out here, I don't think anyone knows what's going on, so you'll be starting even." Mark grabbed my shoulders and pointed me toward the front door of operations. "You guys have fun." Then, he turned and walked away.

Steve introduced us to the operations NCO. "We're here to serve, Sarge," he said.

"Good. There's a chance we're going to be overrun tonight. You guys haul your asses down to the Security Police shack. Do you know where that's at?"

"You bet," Steve said.

"They need every warm body they can find, so get going."
Ol' Sarge was all business.

Steve and I reported to the SP shack and stood around with
a large group of other GIs waiting for instructions. After about
thirty minutes, a major appeared on the steps of the shack and
started barking orders. "Listen up! What I have to say may be the
most important words you will ever hear. They may save your
life." There was intense concern in the man's voice—maybe fear.
"There's a good chance that the enemy'll try to infiltrate the base
tonight. He might even try to overrun it; we don't know. This is
no game. You people are here to make sure that this installation
remains secure. After I'm done here, you'll be loaded on trucks
and taken to various locations around the base. You'll be given
instructions by your squad leaders. Listen to them. Be alert.
Report anything unusual or suspicious. Detain anyone who
doesn't present the proper identification. That's all. Good luck
and be careful."

"We don't know anything about this damn place," I com-
plained to Steve. "I know where the flight line is and I know
where the barracks and mess tent *were*. But, this is one big place,
and I bet we haven't seen half of it."

"Well, I bet we're going to see some new sights tonight,"
Steve predicted.

Several minutes passed. Then a young lieutenant appeared and started loading people onto the trucks. He pointed
to Steve and barked, "You, on this truck!"

Then he pointed at me and said, "You, on that one over
there!"

Steve piped up, "We're together."

"What the hell you mean, 'You're together'? Are you married or something?"

Steve knew there was no use trying to explain. As he
crawled into the back of the truck, I heard him say, "Fuckin'
lieutenants." We'd been a team. We'd never been separated
before. We knew that we could count on one another. Now we
were being sent in different directions with a bunch of strangers.

I crawled into the back of the truck with about a dozen other guys and the truck took off. I didn't say anything to anyone. I just listened to what was being said. The longer I listened, the more concerned I became. These people didn't know what was going on. They had no idea what they were up against and I could tell that they had never done that kind of thing before. They were asking each other questions. And the one or two who were providing the answers were giving the wrong ones. What a zoo! I thought.

The truck finally stopped at a place somewhere between the end of the runway and the sea. A high chain link fence ran in both directions as far as the eye could see. On the base side a dirt road paralleled the fence. Between there and the sea was a large open space filled with elephant grass as tall as the fence. There were guard towers about every five hundred yards or so. It looked like a prison, and I was on the inside.

The truck stopped and I got out. An SP handed me a walkie-talkie and said, "Walk between this tower and that one. Report anything that moves. I'll be by every so often to check, and I'll get something for you to eat later on. Got all of that?"

"Yep. No problem," I said.

After the truck had left and the dust had settled, the world suddenly became calm and quiet, a sharp contrast to the past twelve hours. There was just the rattle of the elephant grass in the evening breeze and the long shadows of the sunset. I pulled a clip from my pocket and poked it into my M-16. I pulled back the bolt and chambered a round. "CLANK!" God, it was noisy! I looked in both directions, trying to make up my mind which tower to approach first. Finally I started walking. I tried to look into the wall of elephant grass, but it was like looking out a screened window. When you focus on the screen, everything beyond is blurred. It was one hundred and fifty-two steps between the towers, and as the shadows faded and the ocean breeze grew cold, after about every ten steps a strange pop or crack came from the wall of grass. With each one, adrenaline ran stronger in my veins, and the breeze grew colder.

Halfway between the towers, on the opposite side of the road from the fence, was a sandbag bunker. When the sun had finally set, I retreated into the bunker and walked in circles holding the walkie-talkie to my ear. It was my link to the rest of the world. Various security points were calling their statuses into the command post. I didn't know where most of the posts were, but I did gather that things seemed to be fairly calm.

As the night grew darker and the breeze grew still, the frogs and night bugs started their nightly chorus. Except for the smell of sandbags, it could have been a peaceful evening anywhere. The darkness hid the reality, and for a while my mind wandered to less tormented times—but never for long. My inner time clock would only let me get away for short periods and then it yanked me back to the present. Each time I hit the present, I felt the same deep inside sadness and a few seconds of grieving. A jeep pulled up and an SP got out and handed me a box lunch. "How are things looking?"

"Nothing happening so far, but who the hell knows what's out there. You can't see your hand in front of your face. Are we going to get some light out here pretty soon?"

"They're going to start kicking flares soon, so keep your eyes open. Okay?" The SP got back in the jeep and headed to the next bunker.

As the jeep's taillights disappeared, the first flare popped into the sky and started its slow waltz to the ground. First there was one, then two and sometimes three. And as each one's light began to fade, another took its place. They filled the sky with light, but at the same time created shadows on the ground that seemed to move and dance to the same tune as the slowly revolving flares. The wail of an F-4 Phantom's engines echoed off the distant mountainsides again and again until the mournful sound finally died. Then the frogs and night bugs became quiet.

"We've got them inside the wire! I repeat, we've got them inside the wire!"

I didn't hear all the transmission, just that someone was

inside the wire—but where? I started playing with the safety on my M-16. Click-automatic, click-semi-automatic, click-safety, click-automatic, click-click-click. The adrenaline was really pumping. My body was tense. A ringing in my ears kept changing pitch and tone. I couldn't stop drying my hands on my pant leg. The sound of automatic weapons filled the air off to my right, and not too far off. I turned and looked in the direction of the fire, but I couldn't see anything. I pressed the walkie-talkie to my ear, but I didn't hear anything. Everything was quiet again.

Clank-clank-clank! I didn't pay attention to the noise at first, but all of a sudden my ears told me that it was new. It was the sound of chain link fencing banging against steel posts. A new flare popped, and two shadows ran across the road. I keyed the walkie-talkie and screamed, "Post number 10, two inside the fence!"

"We're on our way!"

Click-automatic. I turned around three hundred and sixty degrees. Then I did it again. A chant started in my mind. "Watch your backside. Watch your ass. Watch your front. Watch your backside!"

I smacked the clip in my weapon—"It's okay!"

I checked the bolt—"Cocked!"

I fastened the chinstrap on my helmet and watched the shadows. Two more ran across the road, then another. Pop-pop-pop, and the M-16 recoiled into my shoulder. The fourth shadow rolled on the ground. I jumped from the bunker and ran toward it. It got up. This time, the shadow had a face, with terrorized, angry eyes. The young man, about eighteen or nineteen years old, had an AK-47 trained on me. I pulled the trigger on my weapon and held it there. The young man fell backward into the fence, his body thrashing and banging against the fence with the impact of each bullet. He finally fell into the road under the headlights of a jeep. I took my finger off the trigger.

The SP in the jeep looked down at the young man and asked, "How many were there?"

"Six, counting this one. The others headed in that direction," and I pointed toward the flight line.

"They won't get far," the SP responded.

I don't know why, but I walked over to the young man lying on the ground and stared down at him. He stared back at me with fear and pain. Blood mixed with saliva ran out the corner of his mouth, and blood ran from his nose down his cheek. His chest made a hollow, whistling sound with each heavy breath. A gurgling sound came from his throat as he slowly drowned in his own blood. His right hand kept reaching out for something to hold on to. But there was nothing there. I stood and watched until the hand went limp and the whistling stopped. He twitched and life left his body. His eyes stared back at me even in death. I had killed another human being. I had ended a life.

I don't remember much about the next few hours other than walking back to the bunker and leaning against it as the SPs loaded the body into the back of the pickup. I stood there maybe a minute or maybe an hour. I must have done my job because I was there until sunrise.

There are two great fears about fighting in a war. One is dying, the other is killing. I had faced both that night and all I could feel was numb relief. I tried reliving the moment of killing and dying in my mind, reliving the fear. I was not supposed to feel numb. I was supposed to feel anger and fear, outrage and disbelief. But I didn't. I was sure that the dead boy had crawled inside of me and would live there the rest of my life, but I couldn't face him right then.

There was a slip of paper in my wallet from when I was in high school. On it was part of a poem: "No man is an island, entire of itself; every man is a piece of the continent, a part of the main; if a clod be washed away by the sea, Europe is the less, as well as if a promontory were, as well as if a manor of thy friends or of thine own were; any man's death diminishes me, because I am involved in mankind; and therefore never send to know for whom the bell tolls; it tolls

*for thee." I believed what John Donne had written. It was my
creed; it was my honor. It was a path to follow. But now the
path was blurred. I was diminished, and there were no bells
tolling.*

On the wall above the fireplace in my parents' living
room is a framed copy of the Declaration of Independence.
*Beside it is a bust of Thomas Jefferson. To me, that man and
that document are the essence of America. The assertion that
all people have a God-given right to life, liberty, and the
pursuit of happiness was my heritage and I was proud of it.
The castoffs of the world had come together and raised the
consciousness of humanity, believing that their country had a
mission to enlighten the world, to eliminate pain and hunger,
to take the bird with the broken wing and nurse it until it
could fly. That was what I believed America was about. That
was what I was about.*

But I discovered that what I believed was not the dream
of all the people. I remember standing by the highway in my
hometown with some of my friends as a black man came
walking down the road. My friends and I watched as he
passed by. He stopped at the town pump for a drink, and one
of my friends remarked, "That nigger had better be out of
town by sundown."

"Why?" I asked.

"That's the law."

"Why?"

"Because they're not like us."

"Have you ever known one?"

"No. And I don't want to know one. I hate niggers."

I couldn't figure the logic. If I was to hate someone or
something, I would want to understand why. Ignorance and
fear go hand in hand. When people don't understand something, they have a tendency to fear it. I guess I always turned
everything around—my greatest fear is ignorance. What my
country was doing in Vietnam was ignorant, and I was a part
of it.

Da Nang, Vietnam—February 1968

I met Steve that afternoon at base operations. He could tell by the expression on my face that something was wrong, and asked, "What happened last night? You look like hell."

I didn't really feel like talking about what happened. I don't think I *could* have talked about it, so all I said was, "I killed a boy last night."

Steve put his arm around me and in a soft voice said, "Oh." We walked out the front door of the operations building and sat on a stack of empty pallets, looking at the mountains at the far side of the flight line. "Mark says we're going back to Korat," he said.

"For what?" I asked.

"For good," Steve replied. "They don't want us around here anymore."

"What are we going to do back there?"

"I guess we'll go back to turning wrenches," Steve answered.

I didn't say much else. I just thought to myself that it would be nice to go back to doing the same old boring job every day. Not worrying about anything, just getting up in the morning, going to work, coming home, taking a shower, going to a movie, writing a letter home, and going to bed.

Mark found us sitting on the pallets daydreaming. "It's your lucky day, boys," he said, waving a couple of letters over his head. "Mail's here."

He handed one letter to Steve and the other to me. I opened mine and two pictures fell out and floated to the ground. I knew what they were as soon as I bent over to pick them up. "I'm a father!" I declared, holding a picture in each hand. I just sat there and looked at the pictures. There was a little wrinkled 'me' wrapped in a blanket. Mark and Steve started dancing around and laughing.

"Congratulations, you son of a bitch!" Mark said, pounding me on the back.

"Read the goddamn letter! Read the letter!" Steve kept repeating. "What is it?"

I unfolded the letter and read the first few lines. "It's a girl. I have a daughter, Shelley Ann." I folded the letter back up and put it in my pocket. I wanted to read it when I was alone. Somehow, I always felt closer to the people I loved when I was alone. So after lunch, I found a shade tree behind the hangar and sat down with my letter. My wife had written it several days before my daughter was born, putting blanks in where the important information would go. My sister-in-law filled in the blanks and mailed it as soon as the baby was born.

Dear Daddy,

I finally came! I'm sure you're anxious to know about me. I weighed 7 lbs. 10 oz. and was born at 1:25 p.m. on Jan. 13. Mom went to the hospital at 9 a.m. on Jan. 13. She is fine. They bundled me up in blankets, put me in a crib, so I guess I'm supposed to go to sleep. Goodbye for now.

Your daughter,
SHELLEY ANN

I sat there under the tree for a long time trying to figure out what was going on. I had just taken a life, and I had created one. Somehow, I *wanted* it all to balance out—life for death, good for bad, happiness for sorrow. I needed some kind of penance to purge my life of this evil, because fathers shouldn't be evil. Someday I wanted my daughter to understand. New fathers were not supposed to be half a world away killing people. They're supposed to be painting the nursery, not sitting alone on a pile of dusty red dirt looking at pictures of their baby. They should be passing out cigars. But most of all, they shouldn't dread the question, "Daddy, where were you when I was born? What were you doing there?"

Steve left for Thailand two days before I did. He was having trouble getting the papers he needed so Kay and her daughter could emigrate to the United States. The Thai government would let Kay leave, but not her daughter. It was a screwed-up mess.

Mark and I were the only ones left. Doc was gone, Tom was gone, and finally Steve was gone. It was a lonely feeling. We hated every moment we were together because we hated everything we'd done and we couldn't wait for the day when it all came to an end. But there was also a great deal of mutual respect and dependence between us, a kind of brotherhood that was never defined or discussed. We lived each other's problems, and shared each other's fears. We had been mad and we had fought, we had cried and held one another. And there were times when we had each needed to be alone.

Doc had told me one time, "I've never been as close to any group of people in my life as I am with you guys, and never as far away." He was talking about the wall that everyone puts up because of the inner feeling that one day you shouldn't get too close to someone—he may be killed. The longer you know someone, the more the wall falls away. If he dies, you rush to put the wall back up; but by then, it's too late. After a while, you learn to make a few holes in the wall or to reach over the top. You don't let it fall down.

Mark knew about the wall. He was on his third tour in Vietnam. No one could get close to him. When I first met him, all I saw was this cold, all-business, black army captain. He represented something I hadn't encountered before. I knew nothing about the army, and I didn't know any black men. I knew I didn't care much for officers. After a few days, none of that seemed to matter. Mark moved smooth and even. He never got in a hurry, he seldom raised his voice, and nothing rattled him. He was always in charge. He earned our respect.

The last night we were in Da Nang, Mark and I sat on a patio drinking a few beers, talking about the past five months. It was the only time he ever opened up. I guess he figured it didn't matter anymore. Our relationship was about to end, so he didn't have to maintain the wall.

"Steve said they're sending you to Cam Ranh Bay," I said.

"Yep, S-4, procurement. They're taking me out of the field."

"Well, that sounds like a good deal."

"Not really, it's a dead end. Can't make rank pushing papers."

"What good is rank if your ass gets shot off? You plan on making this man's army a career? You're going to be a goddamn lifer?"

"Hey man! I never had it so good. I don't exactly come from a middle class background. Not too many bankers live in south Philly. We had rats for house pets, and every morning we had to shove the winos and whores off the front stoop before we could go to school. Shit, a skinny black kid ain't got a chance there. What would you do if every time you wanted to talk to your old man, you'd have to search the alleys and dumpsters? And when you did find him, he was passed out and smelled like shit? My older brother runs numbers, and my little sister is a hooker—real outstanding people. After I had the shit kicked out of me for the two-hundredth time, I decided I would get the hell out of there no matter what it took. I got decent grades in high school, and this army recruiter said he could get me into ROTC if I went to college. So I went for it, and here I am. Like I said, I've never had it so good."

"You went to college. Couldn't you get a good job on the outside?"

"The facts of life are, kid, on the outside a black man can't make the money I'm making. I've got eight years in and three tours. I figure I'm good for major next cycle. One of these days, this war's going to be over and the rank is going to dry up. You have to make it while the making's good."

I looked Mark in the eye and said, "I can't look at this war in a dollar and cents way. Besides, I don't make shit and I can't wait to get the hell out of here."

"I'm Army. I'm in for twenty. After that, I join the rest of you and sit back in my easy chair and pass judgment on world morality. Until that time, I'll stay a tool of Uncle Sam. I agree that this war sucks, that the generals don't know how to fight it. Hell, most of them are still fighting World War II. I'm good at what I do, and someday there may be another war, a just war, and I'll be needed."

"You mean that you can go through every day not letting this place get to you?" I asked. "You don't stop and wonder if you are doing right or wrong? I can't do that, I can't separate myself from my conscience."

"You live in a good and a bad world," Mark answered. "*You* want to believe that man is by nature good. *I* say man is by nature neither good nor bad. *You* want to believe that man is guided by rules and logic. *I* say that rules and logic have nothing to do with it. Fear rules the whole mess, no matter how insane it is. That's what it's all about, running from fear or fighting fear. People still think there's a sabertooth tiger outside the cave. Try to take a bottle from a wino, and he sees the tiger. Walk on a neighbor's lawn, and he sees the tiger. If you take the rice bowl from one of these gooks, he sees the tiger. That's what this war is all about—the tiger. It doesn't make any difference if the tiger exists. People can't live without it. They get all screwed up in the head when they're not scared. There are all kinds of modern names for it—ambition, drive, image, place in the community, status, technology, the bomb. You name it, it all comes back to the tiger.

"When I left the first time, I was just a grunt. I'd spent thirty-two weeks out in the bush as a recon for the 101st. For a whole year, I was crawling around out there." Mark kept pounding the table with his index finger and looking toward the mountains.

"For a whole year, I sweat my ass off wading around in that slop, digging the mud out of my ears and the leeches out of my skin. Search and destroy, search and destroy. Find the little fuckers and kill them before they kill you. I never felt more alive. It was the edge man, the razor's edge. My body used to ache just from the intensity of trying to stay alive. My eyeballs hurt from being open too wide, my jaw hurt from clenching my teeth. I found out what my limits were, and then I went beyond them. I was good, man, I was fuckin' good. I'd never been so good at anything in my life. I only lost four guys out of my platoon in that whole year, only four fuckin' guys. Do you know how good that is?"

I didn't answer. Something in his voice, the intensity or the anger, told me it was better just to listen.

"When I got back to the 'world,' they parked me behind a desk at Fort Bragg, and I began to die. Hell, the whole place was dying. The whole world was on a death march. You know what I mean?"

"No." I had no idea.

"Well, it's like nobody really lives. There are just a short few seconds when you are first born, those seconds when you are fighting for your first breath and screaming your head off; that's when you are alive. But, as soon as they stick a tit in your mouth, that's when the long downhill slide begins. You become dependent, man. They got you by the balls."

"Tits seem pretty natural to me. I've seen some I'd like to be dependent on." I tried to add a little humor, but Mark didn't respond to it.

"It ain't the tits, man. It's like my mother, she's been dying for fifty years. Everyday's a bitch. She ain't never had any money. The power company was always shutting off the lights, the landlord was always pounding at the door, and the old man was always beating on her. Someday, I'm going to get her out of there. But, it won't make any difference—she's given up. I can make sure the old man stays away, and I can give her a nice place to live, but it won't make any difference. She's dying. She's got no control, she's got no dreams, she's dependent."

"Well, maybe if you get her out of that environment, she'll change. She might surprise you. Maybe there are still some dreams alive inside her."

"You don't get it man! She's been that way too long. She's set her limits. She parks in front of a color TV and that's as far as her dreams go. There's a whole world out there like her, slowly dying in front of a TV.

"I ain't going to be that way. I'm going to stay alive. When I was back at Fort Bragg, I started to die. All I did was shuffle paperwork—fill out forms and move them from one basket to another. When I was done, I went to the same bar and had a few drinks, went home with the same lady, and passed out in the same bed. Life was over for me. I'd had my chance. I'd had my time in the spotlight. Now, it was my time to start dying."

"Why didn't you get out of the army and find a job? If you were good at this, you've got to be good at something else. I can't believe that in this whole screwed-up world there isn't something that I can't do better than fighting in some stupid war. If this is as intense as it gets, if this is as alive as I'll ever be, then I'll just go blow my brains out tomorrow."

"Hey, man, they've been running a scam on us since the beginning of time. It's always been the dumb ones—the poor city kids and the farm hicks—that have fought the wars. It's the only chance in their whole lives to be heroes. It's their chance to be the Roman Legion or to slay the dragon. It's the one time in their life that they can pick up a newspaper or magazine and say, 'Hey, I was there. I did that.' Then if they don't get killed or go crazy, they can go home, hang their little medals on the wall, and tell war stories while they slowly die. Look around. How many rich kids do you see here?"

"Steve's rich, and he's here. He's been in it just like the rest of us," I answered.

"Steve's different. He comes from people with old-country values. He comes from people who still believe in duty, honor, and country. His people ain't been rich long enough.

"The rich don't fight wars. They've got better and more important things to do. They've got no time for all this shit. They hire guys like us to do it for them and then sit off on the hillside and take bets on the battles. Their lives revolve around power, getting it, keeping it, and using it. They love power, and they'll do anything for it except die for it."

"Sounds to me like they ought to love you," I said, getting

pissed. "You don't learn. You keep coming back. You're doing everything they want. By the way, who the hell are *they*?" I was getting mad, but not at Mark. I was mad because I was starting to believe what he was saying. "You keep talking about *they*. Do you mean the rich, the government, who? Or are *they* your tiger? Are there always going to be the good guys and the bad guys?"

"That's it, man, get pissed." Mark said.

"What does getting pissed do?"

"It keeps your blood pumping. It keeps your mind working. It keeps you alive. It means that you still have the power, the means to change."

"It sounds to me like you are trying to make something philosophical out of war," I said. "All I see is death and misery. I killed a kid the other night. What's philosophical about that?"

"You don't understand, man," Mark said, leaning back in his chair. "Let me see if I can make it clear. I hate war, you hate war. Got that? Okay. There's more than one way to hate this damn thing. You can stand on the outside and scream and holler or you can do something on the inside. We can both sit here from now on and talk about the right and wrong of it all. But the fact remains, this is a war. There will probably always be wars. These are facts of life. Now when you leave here, you can tell the world all about the horrors of war. You can go home and protest and march. But ask yourself, 'What good is it going to do?' I made up my mind back at Fort Bragg that if I wanted to do something about the war, the best thing I could do was be the best damn soldier I knew how. I came back and a lot of young men went home alive because of me. I'm proud of that. I figure that every boy I send home alive is one more person who will hate war. Dead people don't hate wars. People who have never fought in one don't hate war. *You* hate war." Mark pointed his finger at me from across the table.

I pointed my finger back at him and asked, "What about that other bullshit about people slowly dying and the rich and your version of the bogeyman?"

"That ain't no bullshit. That's what I believe. That's the

way I grew up. That's what I saw. Wait until you get a few more years on you. Wait until you get back to the world—you'll see."

I didn't know if Mark was too bitter or a realist. The idea of some unknown force controlling my life was hard to buy. But here I was and I didn't want to be here.

We sat there and stared into our beers for a few minutes. I guess we were remembering the past few months. I finally said, "Doc used to say that there is hope and no hope, and of the two, he preferred hope. It was one of his simpler sayings."

"Yeah, Doc was one messed-up dude," Mark half-laughed, never looking up from his beer.

"Think about it, man," I said. "Think about it."

"Think about what?" Mark looked up from his beer.

"About you, Doc, Steve, Tom, and me. Where are you going to find five people that different? You'd have to really work to find five people from such different backgrounds. Steve's rich, we're poor, you're black, I'm white—you know, different. But we all got along most of the time. In fact, I'd like to think that we really cared for one another."

"Yeah, I love you, too."

"I ain't talking about that kind of bullshit, man!"

"I know," Mark said sheepishly. "I know what you're saying. Don't think for a minute that we would have anything in common if it wasn't for this lousy place."

"That's not the point," I said. "What we found out was that we had more in common than any of us ever thought possible. It was this place that made us see that. You may think I'm being sentimental or mushy, but I'll never forget any of you guys. I learned a lot. How can I forget Doc? He was my father over here. When I would get all messed up, he was the one who picked me up. He was the one who reassured me when I thought I was going crazy. And he was the one who said that it was all right to be scared."

"So what was I? Your mother?" Mark asked, trying to keep it light.

"No, that was Steve. He was the one who cooked and

cleaned. Doc was the father, Steve the mother, and Tom and I were the kids. We were the wild ones, the ones who were always going off half-cocked."

"Then who was I?" Mark looked hurt.

"I don't know for sure, maybe the cops, the priest, someone like that. It doesn't matter. You know, you're the first black man I ever worked with. In fact, you're the first black man I ever really got to know. You're a good leader. You're a good man. And I think behind that stone exterior, there's a man with a big heart." Mark just stared at the mountains. "You know," I said, "maybe there's something to be said for throwing dumb slum kids and dumb hick kids together. Maybe *they* won't be able to bullshit us forever."

Mark stood up and said, "You're learning kid. Let me buy us another beer."

Korat, Thailand—February 1968

I went back to Korat the following morning. As the old C-47 cleared the end of the runway and banked toward Monkey Mountain, I looked out on the large field of elephant grass at the end of the runway. It was swaying in the sea breeze and was full of waves, just like the ocean. My eyes froze on that patch of grass until it was just a brown, blurry speck on the horizon. I guess I was hoping if I stared long enough, it might lead me to some kind of understanding. I was leaving this place, and I still didn't understand why I was there. I didn't understand what I had done.

I always figured that I would know what it was all about before I left. The war wasn't a puzzle. There had to be someone somewhere who had the answers. I'd hoped that that person would come forward and tell me the reason all this was going on. I'd heard all the pat answers, of course. I'd read the papers and listened to the news. But the accounts and the reasons didn't match with the reality I knew. I guess I pictured some mysterious man with sunglasses and a trench coat hiding in the shadows, whispering, "Psssst, buddy, you want the answers?"

Steve was waiting when the plane landed. I was really glad to see him. He said, "Grab your shit, man. I'll help you get settled. We've got important things to do."

"What important things?"

"We've got a new bungalow."

"What do you mean, *we*?"

"You and me, bud, that's who. You and me and Kay and the kids. You've got to see it. It's out of this world."

"You don't want *me* living with you."

"We wouldn't have it any other way. Besides, Kay needs a babysitter while she's at the bank."

"I knew there was a catch."

"Only kidding, man."

"Did you and Kay get all that paperwork taken care of?"

"Hell, I don't know. I went down the other day and extended for another year."

"You did what? You've got to be out of your mind!"

"Hey, I ain't like the rest of you guys. I don't have it so bad. My family's here. Maybe when you see the bungalow, you'll understand. I get up in the morning, go to work, and come home. Kay's got dinner on the table, you know, just like home. Hell, if things don't work out, I might just stay over here."

"What the hell are you going to do over here?"

"Import, export. You've seen all this shit they try to sell us over here. Ship it back and sell it to the rest of the people. You know me. I'll think of something."

I wished that I could look at life the way Steve did. Nothing ever shook him up. If things didn't work one way, he'd try it another way, and if that didn't work, he'd do something else.

After I signed in, Steve and I went down to the maintenance building. I put my tools away and got my work assignments. After some fast talking, I managed to get the swing shift with Steve. I liked working swing shift. There wasn't a lot of bullshit—no big shots run around at night. Night was the time when most of the work needed to be done, and people let you do it.

I got a three-day pass before I had to start work. I needed the time to settle in and get things organized. The first thing was to see the "out of sight" bungalow Steve had rented.

"Well, what do you think?" Steve asked as we rode up to the front gate.

"'Out of sight' describes it, all right," I answered. It was in impressive place, surrounded by a high block wall with huge orange iron gates in front. The bungalow was a big two-story house painted white with orange double front doors. There was orange iron latticework over all the windows, and the roof was covered with orange tile. Someone had really liked orange. There was a front porch, and two balconies extended from the upper floor. At each corner of the house was a huge clay pot to catch the rainwater, and beside each pot grew banana plants. There was no lawn, just red dirt and gravel. Palm trees shaded the back of the house, but the front baked in the sun. The only thing that looked out of place was the log chain wrapped around a porch post.

"What's that for?" I asked Steve.

"That's where we lock up the bikes. Thieves will carry them right over those gates if you don't do something to prevent it."

Inside, the bungalow was just as impressive. The floors and woodwork were all dark shiny teakwood. Everything else was white. Ceiling fans turned slowly in every room and a Thai ballad played softly on the stereo. There was a large bamboo sofa with white cushions covered with large red flowers. Vines and plants hung from all the windows and blocked out most of the midday sun. Kay had a green thumb, and she had gone wild inside the house.

"Goddamn, how much did all this cost you?"

Steve just laughed, "Don't worry about it. It's only money."

"Maybe *you* don't have to worry, but I tend to get this

real fear when my wallet's empty."

"Like I said, don't worry about it. I've got this pipeline back to the world, remember?"

I knew Steve would have his way in the end, so I gave in. "What the hell. Where's my room?"

It was hard the first month or so. Steve and I kept trying to talk, but it was always small talk. We went to Bangkok a couple of times, but always seemed to avoid the old places. We never talked about Mark and Tom and Doc. The conversation was always centered on the present, never the past and never the future. I noticed that whenever Kay started making plans, Steve would get upset and leave the room. The plans weren't anything monumental, just everyday-living kind of plans. Steve couldn't handle them. Kay would stare at me with a confused, hurt expression. All I could do was stare back. I knew what was inside Steve, but I couldn't explain it to Kay. I couldn't even explain it to myself.

On evenings off, Steve and I would sit on the upstairs balcony as the sun was going down and drink too many beers. Hardly talking, we just watched the people go by. As time went on, I noticed that we both had an obsession with the eastern sky. We would sit in the chairs, get up and walk around, and sit back down again. No matter how many times we went through the routine, we always ended up sitting on the eastern railing watching the horizon. I never mentioned it to Steve. I didn't want to get into symbolic psychological bullshit. But I knew what it meant. It had something to do with turmoil and things left undone, both in Vietnam and in our own minds.

Steve and Kay had a fight one afternoon, so I went for a bike ride. When I returned, Kay was gone and Steve was standing on the balcony. I sat down in a chair and picked up a magazine.

"What the hell's wrong with me?" Steve turned around with tears in his eyes. "Ah, goddamn it. I ain't supposed to do this shit!" He turned back around and tried to hide the tears. He didn't say anything for a few moments, neither did I. Then he repeated, "What's wrong with me?"

I didn't say anything. I knew what was coming, but I didn't have any of the answers. "She just needed some money to send to her mother, that's all. A few lousy bucks, and I come uncorked like a crazy man. I've got the money." He reached in his pocket, pulled out some bills, and threw them on the floor.

"I don't talk half the time and the other half, I'm mad." I just sat and listened. "This may sound nuts, but sometimes I see life like a river. There's water upstream and there's water downstream, but right in the middle, there's this big, dry hole with cracked mud in the bottom and fish skeletons scattered all over. It's kind of like when Moses parted the Red Sea, you know, in the movie. There was this wall of water on both sides, and a dry space in the middle. That's what I'm talking about.

"I know what you're talking about," I answered. I walked over to the railing and stood beside Steve. "I don't know what to say. It's kind of like the blind leading the blind. Neither one of us talk much. We wander around like a couple of zombies. Every time we go out in public, we put on these masks and try our damnedest to act normal, but most of the time we don't see or hear what's going on because we're someplace else. We try to use home as a hiding place, but that doesn't work either. When we come home, we take it out on everybody because we know that what we're doing isn't normal. Pretty soon we're pissed at the whole world and the people in it. All I can say is, it's going to take time."

We talked for most of the afternoon. We talked about work, the kids, Kay, the house, and a little bit about the future. But we never talked about Doc, Tom, or the war. Steve and I were the best of friends; we had been since the beginning of this whole mess. We had shared a lot. It's not very often that people can accept each other at any level and are willing to put up with the mood swings and nasty temperament. Steve did, and so did I.

Somehow, we got each other through the next five months. Our friendship wasn't the same as in the beginning. It was more a shared, unspoken understanding. There were both a closeness and a distance. We needed each other to lean on, and the freedom to search for our answers independently.

When July came, my tour in Southeast Asia was up. Steve came into my room the night I was packing. He sat on my bed for several minutes before he said anything. He kept rolling and unrolling a pair of my socks. "I loved Doc," he said, never looking up from the socks. "My momma always said that you make the best friends in the worst times. And now *you're* going. There's no one left. Why does it hurt so much inside? I try to reason it all away, but it still hurts. I ought to be happy for you. You're getting out of this shit-hole."

Before I could say anything, Steve threw down the socks and walked out the door. I was relieved, because I didn't know what to say and I don't know if I could have said it if I did. I heard Steve start his motorcycle and ride off. I never saw him again, and I understand why.

That is what I learned, my father.

United States—July 1968

Leaving Thailand—and Southeast Asia—was one of the most emotional experiences of my life. I was going back to the world; I was going home. It was time to get on with the rest of my life. I kept walking around the airport thinking to myself, "Be cool, everything is going to be all right. This is the day you've been waiting for. It's over."

I kept thinking about my life before the war. I tried to focus on what the war had interrupted. I had a wife and a new daughter waiting, and that meant a home. I had two years left in the Air Force, so that meant a job. On the surface, everything seemed to be in order. All I had to do was go back and get started. But getting started seemed to be my problem. I had to find the starting point, the beginning. There had to be ideas and dreams to start with. And I had no dreams, I had no ideas. I was used to being mechanical, a robot, doing what I was told when I was told. My feelings and emotions had been suppressed, and that was what I was trying to overcome. I knew that I had changed, and that meant explaining a lot of things I couldn't explain, or didn't care to.

As the plane crossed the Pacific, I told myself, "Be calm, be cool. Take things as they come. You can handle it." Then every once in a while, I would switch gears and get mad at myself.

"What the hell are you worried about? You're going home—
HOME, MAN, HOME!" By the time the plane landed at Travis,
I had myself convinced that I could handle the situation. If I
could live through a year of hell, I could handle anything.

On the bus trip from Travis to the San Francisco airport, I
was calm and relaxed; I was proud of myself. But when the bus
arrived at the airport, things started to change. I couldn't take the
crowd. I couldn't stand the people hurrying in all directions,
dressed in different colors, making all that noise. I bought my
ticket and retreated to the relative calm of the boarding area.

I had purchased a military standby ticket, which meant
that I had to wait until all the full-paying passengers checked in
before knowing if space was available. A group of college
students and an Air Force major who also had standby tickets
waited with me. When the last of the full-paying passengers had
left to board the plane, the ticket agent called us all over, saying,
"I've got two seats left."

About that time, a guy I knew from Korat came running
up. "Am I too late?" he asked. "No," I answered. I pushed my
way through the students and past the major to the ticket
counter. "We've got those seats," I told the agent. The man
looked at me then at the crowd standing behind me.

"Well, I don't know, sir."

The major came walking up to the counter and asked
"Airman, what do you think you're doing?"

"Ain't no doubt about it, Major, we're getting on that
plane. We've spent the past twenty hours on a plane and we've
eaten a ton of bullshit. We ain't been home in a goddamn year—
that plane is ours!"

The major backed off, smiled, and said, "Good luck!"

I was ready to fight, and I think the major knew it. I had
always been a passive person, the guy waiting at the back of the
line. The incident took me by surprise, and I was embarrassed.
It showed me who I had been and who I was now. I had had no
control over what had happened. All the plans I had made to act
unchanged went up in smoke. Six hours back in the world and

I already knew that my plans weren't going to work, that I had some problems to deal with. But I was going home, and that was what was important.

Once I was on the plane, I passed out. I hadn't slept in three days. The next thing I remember, the stewardess was shaking my shoulder in Des Moines. The rest of the day was a blur. I remember kissing my wife, Patty, and my mother and shaking hands with my father. I remember I had a sunburn that hurt like hell. I got into my parents' car and thought that I hadn't sat on something so soft or ridden in something so smooth in a long time. I looked out the window trying to find things that had changed in the past year. But most of all, I remember seeing my daughter, Shelley, for the first time. She was standing in her crib at my wife's parents' house. When I walked over and picked her up, she didn't cry; she just stared at me. Then she looked at her mother as though asking, "Who is this stranger?" I set her on my lap. I was expecting some kind of emotional explosion to take place. My mind kept repeating, "She's your baby, she's your daughter!" I was happy and I was proud and I knew that I loved her, but my mind just didn't click the way I thought it would. I guess I was expecting too much.

McConnell Air Force Base in Wichita, Kansas, was my next assignment. I had thirty days to get adjusted to family life and the world in general. Adjustments like sharing a bed, eating real food three times a day, driving on the wrong side of the road, hearing a baby cry in the middle of the night, watching TV, going to stores, not drinking too much beer, driving the speed limit, and most of all, the quiet.

I wasn't alone much during those thirty days, and God, sometimes I needed to be. Everyone was making plans. There was all this "stuff" that had to be done—hurry, hurry. Patty had found a mobile home that she wanted to buy. There were rugs and lamps and dishes and on and on and on. I got into a fight with her one afternoon over the purchase of a washer and dryer, just to get the hell away from it all. I needed some space; I needed to catch my breath.

There is a creek in the pasture behind my parents' house. I always went there when something or someone was bothering me. I would sit under a hickory tree and listen and watch the world go by. It was my "time out" spot. That's where I ended up that afternoon. I walked up and down the creek talking to myself. "She needs a goddamn trailer, she needs a goddamn washer and dryer, she needs this, she needs that. I just came home from a fuckin' war. Doesn't she know that, doesn't anyone know that? Doesn't anyone give a damn? I haven't been out to the market, I've been off blowing other people's brains out, and trailers are important?"

I don't really know what I meant. I knew we needed a place to live. I knew we would be moving in a few days. I guess I was angry because life had not stopped because of the war. I could have walked all over the country and never found a bomb crater, nor one burned-out village. There was no blood. There were no screams. Life went on—an insulated existence away from the pain.

People *knew* about the war. Whenever they found out that I was in the service, they would start in with all their political bullshit reasons why it was wrong for us to be in Southeast Asia—or why it was right, it didn't make any difference. They didn't know what they were talking about. It didn't seem right. I had given all I had to give, and no one noticed, no one cared. A few times I was asked the standard question, What was it like over there? At first, I tried to explain, but when I got to the ugly parts, I was always shut off. The person would shudder, say something like, "Oh God!" and change the subject. It didn't take me very long to develop the pat answer, "It wasn't very nice." They could handle that. I tucked the rest into the back of my mind and hoped that someday, I could use the same answer on myself.

Wichita, Kansas—August 1968

Patty and I moved our trailer to Kansas and I started what would become a twelve-year career with the Air Force. I didn't like the service, but I was good at what I did. No one had ever told me you could be good at something you didn't like. More than anything, I think it was the people that kept me in. All my friends were in the Air Force, so it was an easy place to stay.

In the beginning, I thought I was doing a good job of putting the war behind me. I became caught up in being a husband and father, in providing the best possible life for my family. I worked hard, the promotions came, and so did money and material possessions. The trailer was soon replaced by a house. There were a new car, a color TV, new furniture, and nice clothes—the good life.

My youngest daughter, Heather, was born in September 1970. I stayed with my wife during the whole childbirth. I held my daughter an hour after she was born, not seven months later, as with Shelley. I saw her as a sign that life was good and right. She reinforced my determination to be a good father.

But all that time—when life was good and everything seemed to be coming together—the war started creeping back. At first, it was just bits and pieces, and I passed it off as a normal reaction to the aftermath of war. A sound or a smell would bring back some blurry memory. I didn't like busy or congested places; shopping malls gave me a headache and I couldn't stand in checkout lines.

One night I sat up in bed, awakened by a dream. I can't remember what the dream was about, but Doc was there. It was a dream about a family picnic back in Iowa. Doc didn't belong, but he was there eating a piece of chicken at the end of the table. He didn't say anything, and he wasn't an important part of the dream; he was just there. The dream really upset me. I remember thinking that Doc had invaded my life, and I wanted to know why. I lay there the rest of the night with Doc running through my mind. What did he want, what was he doing?

That was the first dream of many. There were more dreams

of Doc and there were dreams of Farmer Ho and his family. There were dreams of a faceless baby girl and dreams of the boy I'd killed. And as time went on, the dreams started to fill my days, as well. A baby would cry at K Mart, and it would be the faceless little girl. Someone would laugh, and it was Doc. The wind would blow, and I would hear Farmer Ho calling to his children. I never knew when the war would return. Sometimes it was gone for months, but each time it returned, it stayed longer.

As the months passed, reality became distorted. I kept comparing the way I had lived with the way I was living. When I bought a new car, I saw refugees carrying all they owned on their backs. When we moved into a new house, I saw the grandfather and his grandson tearing apart a shipping crate, and people sleeping in cardboard boxes. Buying shoes reminded me of a homeless leper. When my children wouldn't eat all their meal, I thought about the babies that had no food. If the world was a village, the United States was the mansion on the hill, full of rich people with no real problems in life. Their bellies were full, and they didn't get wet when it rained. All they had to worry about was oil spots on the driveway and bugs in the lawn.

When I returned from Southeast Asia, the country was being torn apart by the war. That's what the TV newsman said. The streets were full of protesters. Everyone had an opinion about the war, and students at Kent State died because of it. But no one really wanted to know about the war, the pain and the guilt. No one wanted to know what it was like to wash the blood of a friend from your hands. No one wanted to know about the smell of burning flesh or bloated, decaying bodies. No one wanted to know about the guilt of leaving your friends behind or about not dying yourself. People were afraid to ask what was happening in Vietnam. They were afraid of what it would do to their neatly wrapped sense of morality, of what it might do to the foundation of their mansion. I lived the two worlds. I had seen both sides and could live in neither. I had nightmares about one and no dreams of the other.

Centerville, Iowa—August 1977

In 1977, I got out of the Air Force and moved back to southern Iowa. The war was over and most of my friends were gone. I figured the best thing to do was to go home.

Iowa hadn't changed much, but I had. Putting down roots and watching my family grow seemed like a good idea, and I kept telling myself that that was the place to start over. It was a place where I could grab hold of the past to displace the anxiety of the present.

I got a job and at the end of the week I brought home a paycheck and gave it to my wife. And the next week, I did the same thing. As the weeks turned into months, I learned that I didn't have what it takes to be a success—the drive, the ambition, the sense of importance. My mind was always occupied with small fragments of the past, nothing coherent, disjointed fragments banging around in my brain. All I wanted to do was get away and empty my mind. There was something wrong, and no amount of money could fix it.

I started taking long walks. I would find a lonely dirt road and walk until it ended. Then I'd walk off into a field or the woods. I'd walk until my mind was empty and the fragments stopped banging around. I'd walk until I was exhausted, because exhaustion meant the nightmares wouldn't come. The walking was also an escape from people. I could go to the woods and sit on a tree stump and listen to the silence, the emptiness. I didn't have to make excuses or give reasons. The woods accepted me for who I was, with all my guilt, all my questions, all my doubts. The woods never asked, Why don't you? or Why can't you?

I was a zombie going through the motions of living. I looked around and did what everyone else was doing, only I did it with no reason, no emotion. I just followed whoever was leading—my wife, my children, my family. I made an attempt to do what was expected, when it was expected, in the manner that was expected. When the pressure got too great, I went for a walk.

When I was laid off from a job with the water company, I

went to the woods. I had reached a new low and knew something had to be done. But when I got to the woods, I couldn't
even talk to *myself*. All I could do was empty my mind and stare
into space. I got scared, then furious. I started screaming, "Why
don't they understand? Why don't I understand? I never wanted
to kill anyone. I never wanted to be this way!"

That afternoon was a turning point. All my emotions came
out as anger. I resolved never again to trust another human, to
live my life on my terms and my terms alone. I wouldn't take the
bullshit anymore. I wouldn't live in a bullshit world, where
morality is just a cosmetic surface on society.

Centerville, Iowa—September 1980

During my years in the Air Force I had taken several
college courses. I liked college—it was a place where answers
could be found, a place where people looked deep into the
world. I didn't have any particular goal, I just liked the feeling.
In 1980 I went back to college. My father was a teacher, my
brother went to college to be a teacher, my sister was going to be
a teacher, even my brother-in-law and sister-in-law were teachers. Hell, everyone I *knew* was or had been a teacher.

At first everything went well; I was making the grade. For
the first time in a long while, I felt like I was doing something
worthwhile. Life had direction and a purpose. I was developing
into a good teacher. During student teaching, my students
wanted to learn and we had a good time learning together.

Then one day, I received a letter from the Veterans Ad-
ministration informing me that they were terminating my edu-
cational benefits. They claimed that I had been overpaid twelve
hundred dollars the previous semester due to some kind of
computer screwup. My benefits would not continue until I had
reimbursed them.

A few days later, while in history class, the smug young

professor was talking about Vietnam. The war had been over only five years, but I was amazed at how uninformed the students were. Some laughed and called it "the war we lost" while others thought we should go back and win. The professor spotted me sitting in the back of the room and said, "James, you're a vet. Tell us what Vietnam was about."

I picked up my books, stood up, looked at the class, said, "It was about twelve hundred dollars," and walked out of the class—and college.

Centerville, Iowa—September 1982

I became the caretaker of Oakland Cemetery in Centerville, the local gravedigger. There was an odd sense of peace about the job, a limbo between the living and the dead, a place where time had no meaning, where a life was clearly defined by two dates carved into rock. I hoped it was a place to start again, where I could grasp the few fragments of what I thought was reality and find some peace in life. But the anger and the guilt wouldn't go away. Reason and logic were no match for them. The peaceful green hills of Oakland Cemetery couldn't overcome them.

After a while the anger overcame the guilt. It grew and became a wedge between myself and the world around me. My walks were longer and more intense. I'd walk until I could walk no more. Or I'd get on my motorcycle and ride until my legs and hands grew numb. I isolated myself from everyone I loved and who loved me. I wanted to explain what was going on inside me, but I couldn't because I didn't know myself. All I knew was that I didn't fit in. I was always on the sidelines watching; my emotions and mind didn't fit the grooves.

Around Christmas 1984, I began to dream about the young man I had killed at Da Nang. I don't know why he came back; he just showed up one night and wouldn't go away. At first, he just peeked around the corners in my dreams, but it wasn't long before he filled my nights. I tried to get away from him by not sleeping, but he found a way to invade my days. I couldn't get away from him. He crawled inside me and made me ask questions that I never wanted to ask, questions that I knew no answers to, questions that would make him a part of me forever. Each night I flooded my mind with other thoughts to keep from answering the questions. The next day, the questions would still be there, just below the surface. I kept telling myself, "Put it off. You don't need this shit now. It won't do any good. Save it for a time when you are away from this place. Put it away until a time when it won't hurt."

One night I drove my truck far from my house. It was very cold, and the snow was new and deep. The moon was bright and the woods were full of shadows and silhouettes. I felt more alone than I had ever felt in my life. I had driven the wedge home, and there was no one left. I began to sob, "Who were you? What was your name?" It all came pouring out—all the guilt, all the anger, all the pain. I think I went crazy that night.

The next two days were a blur. I remember having a fight with my wife, telling my brother and father that I had killed someone, and driving and driving and driving. I remember walking and running through the woods, sweating, and that my chest hurt. On the third day I went to the hospital and learned I had had a heart attack.

I spent seven days lying in the hospital, being watched by people who treated me like a broken Humpty Dumpty. They all huddled around trying to figure out a way to put me together again. I felt like a trapped animal. A voice inside kept saying, "Mister, you've reached the end of your rope. You are killing yourself."

At the time, I didn't much care if I lived. I didn't really want to die, but life was a major pain. Lying in a hospital bed didn't make the anger go away. The threat of my mortality didn't answer my questions; in fact, it added many more. I couldn't stand the line of people coming and going from my room. They cared about me, but I didn't *want* them to care. That's the part that bothered me. I just wanted to get out of that bed and disappear down some dirt road as soon as I was better.

I spent the next two years turning myself into a hermit. That's not what I had planned to do, but that's what happened. After the heart attack, I tried to put some reason into my life. I tried to start over, to back up and begin again. But there was no one there to start with. I was a stranger to everyone I knew. All the people I loved no longer believed in me or trusted me.

After a while I moved to the woods and lived in a tent. When it got too cold, I made myself a room in an abandoned corncrib. At night, I would walk the woods and listen to the night sounds. The owls and the wind became my friends. For the first time in a long time, I had friends. It was the first time in a long time that I wanted friends.

I sat in that corncrib and tore myself apart. At the end of the line, I had one of two choices. I could walk out into the cold night and never return, or I could walk back into the world. Deep inside I knew that I didn't have the guts to kill myself, so that left me with only one possibility, to rejoin the world of the living, which scared me more than dying. I had two daughters whom I deeply loved, but I didn't show that love. They had grown up never really knowing their father. They just knew a very angry man who lived at their house once in a while.

My wife was a beautiful, kind, strong lady, but our lives had always seemed to go in opposite directions. Through all my problems, however, she had stood by me and watched, and hurt, always there. In those cold nights the only thing that had kept me warm, the only thing that kept me from giving up, was the memories of the few good times we had shared, the realization that somewhere in the bleak world a thread held us all together. Even at the worst of it, that thread—the love of my wife—had never broken.

I walked out of the corncrib and went home.

Welcome home, my son.

Centerville, Iowa—March 1986

There is an old tale about a princess who had her coachman drive her to the market each morning. At the market, she would fill her carriage with loaves of bread. Her coachman would then drive her to a nearby village where she distributed the bread among the poor and starving peasants. One morning, a stranger passed through the village while she was in the midst of her charity. When she offered the stranger a loaf of bread, he refused saying, "No thank you, my lady. Knowledge is my hunger. Why do you hand out bread to these lowly people?"

The princess answered, "It makes me feel good, and God is watching."

And then the stranger asked, "My lady, would there be bread if God was not watching and it didn't make you feel good?"

"That is not the point," she told the stranger. "A princess has always handed out the bread."

Like the princess, I had thought life had preset rules. If I followed those rules, I would feel good and please God. It was that simple.

Eat your oatmeal, you'll grow up strong and healthy.
Always tell the truth.
Study hard so that you can get a good job.
You get out of life what you put into it.

The list was passed down from generation to generation.
No one gave much thought to what these sayings meant. It
was just assumed that good parents repeat them. More often
than not, they were used to evoke a desired response from a
child. The problem arises when the child begins to internalize
them.
If your mother knew you were doing . . .
God is watching . . .

Then one day, the grown child stands by and watches
someone kill a family. On another day, the grown child burns
down someone's home.

If your mother knew . . .

On still another day, the grown child pulls a trigger and
takes a life.

God is watching . . .

The world revolves around crime and punishment, good
and evil, guilt and innocence. Little attention is paid to truth
and understanding. Doc used to say, "Man doesn't have any
control over truth. He may have named it, but he can't control
it. It's metaphysics man, mystic, cloudy, hard to find, but it's
out there."
I wasn't a philosopher, but I knew one thing. Life wasn't
too bad before the war—that was the truth. The old adages
worked until that time. Then they went down the drain. Like
the princess, I did what was expected; I lived by the rules.
And, like the princess, I overlooked the purpose of it all, the

starving peasants. I was angry at what the war had done to me. I felt guilt, not because of what I had done, but because there was no punishment. All the rules had been turned around. Good was evil, evil was good; I couldn't tell the difference.

I had nearly frozen to death in that corncrib. It was my version of going to the mountain. I didn't speak to God, nor did I learn the essence of life, but I did acquire some knowledge and understanding. I killed a young man in Vietnam, and I created two beautiful ladies in the United States. I love them all. And *morning glories still grow among the peas.*

James Seddon is a native of Iowa, and a U.S. Air Force veteran who served in Vietnam and Southeast Asia. He has two grown daughters, Shelley, a prelaw student, and Heather, an artist. He presently lives in Centerville, Iowa, with his wife, Patty. He is currently working on a book of poetry and a novel about life in southern Iowa.